More books by

THE *I CHING*
The Book Of Changes And How To Use It.

I CHING WISDOM
Guidance From The Book Of Changes

A TALE OF THE *I CHING*
How The Book Of Changes Began

THE *I CHING*
Computer Version

I CHING READINGS
Interpreting The Answers
(available Fall 1996)

All books, except for *The I Ching*, are also available on audio tape and CD. All of wu wei's products and ordering information are listed on the world wide web. See page ii for information, or call 800-266-5564.

I CHING
LIFE

LIVING IT

By *wu wei*

Power Press
Los Angeles, California

I CHING LIFE

LIVING IT

By *wu wei*

Power Press, Box 66401, Los Angeles, CA 90066.
Telephone: (310) 392-9393 Fax: (310) 392-7710.
Website: http://www.earthlink.net/~wuwei.
Email to *wu wei*: wuwei@earthlink.net.

Library of Congress Card Number: 95-68319
ISBN: 0-943015-10-3
Copyright © 1996 Power Press
First Edition
10 9 8 7 6 5 4 3 2

Table of Contents

Author's Note viii

Author's Apology ix

Acknowledgements ix

Forward x

A Brief History of the *I Ching* xiv

Chapter 1: On the Wings of Six Dragons 1

Chapter 2: The Greatest Deed 4

Chapter 3: The Dna Molecule, The Binary
    System, And The *I Ching* 6

Chapter 4: The Joyful Journey 13

Chapter 5: Living the *I Ching* Life 25

Chapter 6: Cause And Effect 45

Chapter 7: Fate 52

Chapter 8: Relationships 65

Chapter 9: Integrity And Fear 88

Chapter 10: The God Game 97

Chapter 11: Time, Eternity And Us 105

Chapter 12: Children 114

Chapter 13: Work 129

Chapter 14: Gain and Loss 138

Chapter 15: Recovery 147

Chapter 16: Health 154

Chapter 17: Business 162

Chapter 18: Wealth 176

Chapter 19: Stillness 188

Chapter 20: Personal Goals 196

Chapter 21: Death 208

Chapter 22: Words, Deeds, And Intent 212

Chapter 23: The Superior Person 222

Index 237

Author's Note

The concept upon which this book is written is that the Universe is alive and aware.

The premise upon which this book is written is that by using the *I Ching* we can communicate with the Universal Intelligence which permits us to lead better, fuller lives filled with abundance and well-being. That we can control our destinies and that we can, by taking the appropriate action, enjoy a lifetime of great good fortune and supreme success, are basic assumptions upon which this book is built.

I recommend the use of yarrow stalks in conjunction with *I Ching* divination. For complete instruction for their use, see *The I Ching* by *wu wei*. Yarrow stalks are available through the publisher, Power Press, whose address, telephone number, and internet address for ordering and information appear at the front of this book.

Author's Apology To Women Readers

I sincerely apologize for using *he, his, him* when speaking generally. Using *he/she* throughout becomes cumbersome for the reader and disturbs the flow of thought. I chose to use the masculine form because it is what we are accustomed to seeing in print and because the goal is to make the reading easy.

Acknowledgments

The publisher wishes to acknowledge the meticulous editing of Les Boston of the Boston World Works, Sherman Oaks, California.

The publisher wishes to acknowledge Deborah Glass McFarland of Los Gatos Productions, Venice, California, for her skill and creativity in the layout and design of this book.

Forward

The information in this book has been set forth with one goal: to enable you to lead a better, fuller, easier, more productive life, free from the pitfalls that may have earlier beset your path. It is intended to be a guide, showing you the way to be what the *I Ching* describes as "a superior person" and to suggest ways to use the *I Ching* to accomplish your goals.

Why should you want to follow the life of a superior person? Because of the law of cause and effect that states: "Every action produces a result and the result is in perfect accord with the action." Therefore, if you live the life of a superior person as described within these pages, you will naturally achieve a life of peaceful harmony, having what you want and being who you want. Your path will be straight, the wind will be fair, and your progress will be as an eagle in full flight.

I have written an earlier book called *I Ching*

Wisdom, in which are set forth some of the volatile sayings from the *I Ching*. I use the word "volatile" because one the meanings of volatile is "having the power to fly." These volatile sayings in the *I Ching* will give you the power to fly, will give you the power to break loose from that which holds you, will empower you to reach lofty goals, will provide the means for you to soar to the heights of success, and will show you how to avoid the pitfalls that beset the path of the unenlightened.

In *I Ching Wisdom*, after each saying, there is written a comment that expands the meaning of the saying to help you grasp the wisdom contained therein. Because the sayings in *I Ching Wisdom* demonstrate the function of Universal laws, I have found it useful to reproduce in *I Ching Life* those sayings and comments which elaborate certain basic concepts that are to be found in each of the chapters of *I Ching Life*. For those of you who have read *I Ching Wisdom*, I humbly offer my apologies for the repetition, but my poor mind could find no better words to express some of the great truths than those already used.

In *I Ching Wisdom* it states:

> ### Knowledge
> ### is the key to freedom.

wu wei's comment:

> Knowing how to earn a living frees you from poverty. Knowing how to keep healthy frees you from sickness. Knowing how to entertain yourself frees you from boredom. Knowing the path of the superior person frees you from misfortune, failure, and suffering.

The knowledge that you will gain from living life according to *I Ching* precepts is knowledge that is now coming to you from across the span of thousands of years. It is the knowledge that has been carried to you in a direct line from the great Chinese sage who created the *I Ching*, *Fu Hsi*. The knowledge has sustained your predecessors, sustained their very lives and carried them to the greatest heights attainable in world affairs and personal life. Emperors and common folk alike who have possessed this knowledge have savored the best that life has to offer and have gone on their ways, fulfilled and happy, content as a puppy after drinking his fill of his mother's warm, nourishing milk.

A Brief History of the *I Ching*
(pronounced yee jing)

Thousands of years ago, before the dawn of written history, legend has it that there lived a great Chinese sage known as *Fu Hsi*. It is said that he was the man who first united all of China, becoming her first emperor. He is also credited with leading the Chinese people from the age of hunting and fishing into the age of agriculture.

A man of incredibly vast intellect, *Fu Hsi*, over a period of time and in stages, conceived of a mathematical model of the Universe, complete with all its conditions and elements of change, the sixty-four six-line figures which English speaking people call hexagrams and the Chinese call "*kua.*" (The complete story of how this author believes *Fu Hsi* created the sixty-four *kua* and sent the wisdom on its way through the ages can be found in his book, *A Tale Of The I Ching.*)

Legend has it that in forming the sixty-four *kua* of the *I Ching*, *Fu Hsi* surveyed the vast diversities and movements under heaven, saw the ways the movements met and became interrelated, saw the ways their courses were governed by eternal laws. He thought through the order of the outer world to its end and explored his own nature to its deepest core. He perceived the beginning of all things that lay unmoving in the beyond in the form of ideas that have yet to manifest themselves. He put himself in accord with those ideas and, in so doing, arrived at an understanding of fate.

Writing did not exist at the time of *Fu Hsi*, so his teachings were handed down in the oral tradition, one generation faithfully teaching another, perhaps for a thousand years or more.

When writing began in China five thousand years ago, about the year 3,000 B.C., the *I Ching* teachings were first recorded. Two thousand more years passed, during which time the *I Ching* and its teachings flourished.

In the twelfth century B.C., the tyrant, *Chou Shin*, ruled. He was to be the last emperor of the *Shang Dynasty* (1766-1121 B.C.). He was a cruel and heartless man who tortured people to pleasure himself and his equally cruel and sadistic concubine. So cruel was he that all of China lived in fear of him.

At the same time there also lived a man named *Wen*, a learned *I Ching* scholar of rare insight, who governed a small province in a remote area of western China. *Wen* governed his people according to *I Ching* principles and was, therefore, as much loved and respected by the people as *Chou Shin* was hated and feared. The people urged *Wen* to gather an army and overthrow the tyrant, assuring him that everyone would willingly follow him. *Wen* said that since he was truly a law abiding citizen, he could not take action against the emperor.

Chou Shin heard the rumors that *Wen* was being asked to gather an army to rise against him and had *Wen* arrested and put into prison.

Wen was allowed to live, but only because of his great popularity.

During the year 1143 B.C., the year that *Wen* was in confinement and in fear for his life, he used the *I Ching*'s great wisdom and its divinatory powers to keep himself alive. In *Wen's* time, there were two versions of the *I Ching*: *Gai Tsung* and *Lien San,* and during his time of isolation, he re-interpreted the names of the *kua* and other portions of the great books. He also changed the order of the *kua* established by *Fu Hsi* to the order currently in use in every known version of the *I Ching*. The order in which the *kua* appear does not in any way affect the readings.

In 1122 B.C., *Wen*'s oldest son, *Yu,* after publicly denouncing *Emperor Chou Shin* in order to turn public opinion hotly against him, gathered an army and overthrew the tyrant and became king. The new king, to honor his father, bestowed upon him the title of "King," and he was forever after known as *King Wen*, even though he never ruled as king. *King Yu* died a few years after becoming king, leaving a thirteen-year-old son as heir to the throne. The inexperienced youngster was obviously incapable of ruling, so *King Wen*'s younger son, *Tan*, known as the *Duke of Chou*, ruled in his stead. *King Wen* had instructed *Tan* in the teachings of the *I Ching*, and it was *Tan* who, during his reign as acting king, interpreted the meanings of the 384 individual lines of the *kua*. The *I Ching* was then considered complete. The year was 1109 B.C.

So profound was the wisdom of *King Wen* and his sons, wisdom of the *I Ching* that had been taught in their family for countless generations, that they were able to provide a foundation for their dynasty so strong that it lasted for 800 years, the longest in the history of China.

Several hundred more years passed, and finally, in 551 B.C., the great sage and scholar, *Confucius*, came on the world scene. In his later years he began the study of the *I Ching* and when he was past the age of seventy humorously commented, "If some years were added to my life, I would give fifty to the study of the *I Ching*, and might then escape from falling into great errors."

Confucius wrote many commentaries to the Book of Changes, most of which are reproduced in other versions of the *I Ching*, notably, that wonderful book published by Princeton University Press, Bollingen Series XIX, the Wilhelm/Baynes translation. Should you become so engaged with the *I Ching* that you wish to go beyond using it as an oracle and begin studying it as a book of wisdom, you will surely want to consult that most thorough and profound work.

CHAPTER ONE

ON THE WINGS OF SIX DRAGONS

"The same intelligent, aware force that created and sustains the Universe, which *is* the Universe, created and sustains us. That intelligent, creative, aware force endlessly shapes and alters us, changes us, to the purpose that we will ultimately come to achieve our true nature and thereafter will keep us forever resonating with the great harmony."

-Wisdom of the I Ching

You might well ask, "How long will it take me to achieve my true nature? Ten years? Twenty? A lifetime? A hundred lifetimes? Ten thousand?" The answer is different for each of us, but, by keeping in mind what the goal is: the achievement of our true nature, and by remaining aware that the altering and shaping process through which we will achieve our goal is necessary and entirely for our benefit, we will speed joyously upward to our goal as though on the wings of six dragons.

CHAPTER TWO

THE GREATEST DEED

The greatest deed possible has been accomplished—the creation of the Universe.

Once that deed was accomplished, everything else became possible.

What that means for us is that we can rise to greatness, that we can accomplish our goals, no matter how lofty, that we can be who we want and have what we want, that everything is within our reach.

Is that not wonderful?

CHAPTER THREE

THE DNA MOLECULE, THE BINARY SYSTEM, AND THE *I CHING*

The *I Ching* information has been passed along from person to person for six or seven or more thousands of years. In this, it is no different from any of the other old bits of information and wisdom that have come down to us through the centuries from the people of all the ancient lands.

What makes the *I Ching* stand apart, is that there is substantiation for it in the Universe—physical substantiation. The sixty-four *kua* of the *I Ching* were originally arranged by *Fu Hsi* somewhere between five and seven thousand years ago. This is the order in which he arranged them:

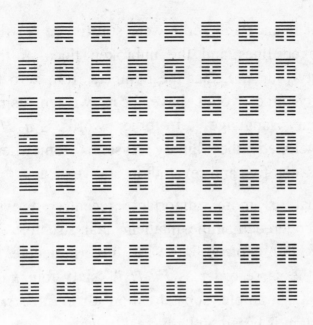

Two hundred years ago, Joseph Leibnitz, a German mathematician, invented the binary system. It is a numerical system, using only zeros and ones, with which any number can be represented, and upon which all computer language is based. Shortly after or shortly before Leibnitz developed the binary system for writing numbers, someone sent him a copy of the *I Ching*. He inspected it and realized that if ones and zeros were substituted for the broken lines and the unbroken lines of the sixty-four *kua*, that the numbers from zero to sixty-three would have been written using binary language. In other words, *Fu Hsi* developed the binary system somewhere between five and seven thousand years ago.

What is more important, recently it was discovered that the mathematical structure of the DNA molecule, the life force molecule, is in the same order as *Fu Hsi*'s sixty-four *kua*. That is ample substantiation that *Fu Hsi*'s system is based on Universal order.

Think of that. With no computers or equipment of any kind, *Fu Hsi* extracted from the Universe a tiny mathematical model of itself. What's even more incredible is that he applied it to the answering of questions. (You may read a full account of how this author believes the *I Ching* came into being in his book, *A Tale Of The I Ching*, Power Press, Los

Angeles, California.)

If you have not used the *I Ching* as an oracle, a source for answering questions with complete accuracy, a brief explanation will make the process clear.

Because we are part of the Universe, and because time is a living entity that contains consciousness—may indeed *be* the consciousness of the Universe, permeating everything, including ourselves—we can know everything the universe knows. All we need is a key to unlock that fount of sublime wisdom and complete information. That we have the key is unquestionable; every time we get a new idea, we have used our key. We like to think that we created the idea, but what we did was no less noteworthy, we channeled the idea from the source; we used our key.

Fu Hsi's sixty-four kua are each made up of six linear lines stacked one above the other as in Fu Hsi's order shown above. The lines can be either broken — — or unbroken ———. Each of the sixty-four kua represents a situation or condition. Within each situation or condition are six lines, each line representing a stage of change. When we ask a question, the answer, which is in the form of a kua, tells us what the situation or condition is that surrounds our question and what to do to achieve a successful outcome or to avoid danger. If there is a moving line, meaning a line or lines that your reading tells you to take into consideration in your answer (fully explained in the *I Ching*), it will give specific guidance about what action to take or not to take to bring about the result that is in your highest and best welfare. The changing line or lines also result in the formation of a new kua which will show you what the result of your actions will bring about.

What is magical about the *I Ching* is not the book itself, the sixty-four kua, but that it provides the key to knowing which kua correctly answers our question. To use this key, we manipulate a bundle of thin sticks called yarrow stalks. The ancient text calls for the use of yarrow stalks, but I have conducted many workshops when we did not have yarrow stalks and instead used bamboo skewers such as are used for barbecuing, and they worked satisfactorily. The Universe will always provide a way for the sincere seeker to obtain answers; however, I strongly advise everyone to obtain yarrow stalks as soon as possible since they are what is specifically called for in the ancient texts. If you cannot get them from your local bookstore, they are obtainable by calling or writing to the publisher listed at the front of the book or by using the publisher's website, also listed at the front of the book.

With the use of yarrow stalks, you can obtain answers to all the questions you can think of— accurate answers—answers that are for your ultimate highest and best good. Is that not wonderful?

CHAPTER FOUR

The Joyful Journey

Every spider web that has ever been woven is different from every other spider web. The face of every person is different from every other face. No leaf that has ever existed has been the same as any other leaf. Everything is different from everything else—the diversification is total. Can you not therefore imagine that the path to enlightenment is different for every person? Must be different? The path that one person follows is not the correct path for any other person. Each of us must follow his own path. That is the way.

You are on your path to enlightenment—you cannot be off your path. The progress you make along your path will be quick or slow according to your level of awareness. By consciously seeking enlightenment, you will progress quickly, receiving the rewards of ever greater enjoyment, peace, success, great good fortune and well-being.

What is enlightenment? It is knowing the truth of your existence. It is knowing who you are in the Universal scheme, and knowing how to live harmoniously within that scheme. To seek enlightenment, hold the goal of achieving enlightenment lightly in your mind—all else will occur as a result of natural law. You might well ask, "How do I hold enlightenment in my mind as a goal?" The answer is: by your desire—your desire to know what your role is in the Universe—your desire to advance along your spiritual path—your desire to live the life of a superior person—your desire to know how others have progressed along the path toward enlightenment. By following those desires, you will, as a result of Universal law, move toward enlightenment.

No one else can walk your path for you. No one else can achieve enlightenment for you. All anyone can do is to point you in the right direction and allow you to do the rest.

Your path, like everyone's, extends to eternity. Be relaxed and cheerful; you are in the perfect hands of the Universe. You're safe. You cannot be hurt in the Universal sense of the word.

When a follower of the *I Ching* way was confronted by a warrior who threatened to cut off his head, the man appeared unafraid, even calm. The warrior asked if he was not afraid of him. The man replied, "I am not afraid of death, why should I be afraid of you?" The warrior threw down his sword and became the man's student.

The path to enlightenment is the path of the superior person. At any moment, including this one, you may set your feet upon that path, radically altering your circumstances and making it possible for you to enjoy the great rewards that are available to everyone, withheld from no one. That you are reading this book is an indication that you are already deliberately on that path. You will find that moving toward enlightenment is a joyful journey.

Using the *I Ching*, you can discover valuable information about your own path to enlightenment and receive specific guidance about ways to traverse that path encountering only great good fortune and sublime success. Is that not wonderful?

You can also protect yourself from danger. That is one of the more important uses of the *I Ching*. Many times in your life you will be threatened by danger. For instance, suppose you have saved some money and are going to spend it to buy a car. Suppose, unknown to you, that money will be needed for another purpose such as a medical emergency. If you were to make an inquiry, asking, what can I expect from my new car purchase, and you received *kua* 29, K'an, Danger, you would know that your purchase would expose you to danger. To find out whether the danger would come from driving the car or from some other source such as the one described above, you would make another inquiry. When you become aware that danger surrounds your purchase of the car, you should pause, determine the source of the danger, and then ask what to do about it.

Suppose you were going to invest in the stock market and received a reading of danger. It would be a wise course of action not to invest in the stock market at that time.

A young man who wanted to purchase a motorcycle asked me for advice. I suggested that he make an *I Ching* inquiry. He made the inquiry asking, "What can I expect from buying a motorcycle at this time?" The answer was *kua* 51, Chen, Shock. The moving line said, "To begin brings danger, to continue brings shock." He wisely did not buy the motorcycle at that time. A year later, he asked again and received a more favorable reading, and so went ahead with his purchase.

A man in California owned a large parcel of real estate which he had to sell because the monthly payments were too much for him and he needed the money for other purposes. He put the property on the market through a broker. An agency of the State of California made an excellent offer to purchase his property. The broker gave the seller the offer from the State of California. Instead of accepting the State's offer, he made a counter offer in which he stated he was not going to sell all of the property as he originally intended, but was going to keep a portion of the property for himself. He sent the altered agreement back to the State. Then he made an *I Ching* inquiry to see if what he had done was the right thing. The answer was *kua* 5, Hsu, Waiting In The Face Of Danger. The moving line, 3, said that he had made a poor start and was only attracting danger. The danger he was attracting was his inability to make the monthly payments if the State did not purchase his property.

The State wrote back to him and said they were not interested in purchasing only a portion of his property. He quickly amended his offer, agreeing to sell all of his property to the State. The State wrote back and said that it was no longer interested in the property.

He would have been smarter to have made his inquiry before replying to the State the first time. He could have asked, "What can I expect if I amend the offer to keep a portion of the property for myself?"

In *I Ching Wisdom* it states:

> *Danger*
> *has an important*
> *and beneficial*
> *use.*

wu wei's comment:

Being aware of danger, you will take the necessary precautions that will protect you from harm when danger arises. By doing this you have used danger to further the achievement of your success and to protect what you already have.

On your path to enlightenment, it is advisable to look for guidance from others whom you admire. Be aware that the path they have followed is their path, not yours. However, they may have useful information you can use for your own benefit. Especially beware of people who call themselves masters or allow others to call them masters. The surest sign that a person is not a master is if he calls himself a master or allows anyone to refer to him as a master. On this earth there are no masters, and each person's journey is unique. That is the way.

In *I Ching Wisdom* it states:

> *Do not allow yourself*
> *to be led astray*
> *by a leader.*

wu wei's comment:

> This is not to say that you should ignore a
> leader or good counsel from a qualified
> person, but that you should question
> whether a leader's course is best or
> honorable for you, and then make your
> own decision.

In seeking advice from others, it is always wise
to listen carefully to what they have to say, but
in the end, you should make whatever decision
you feel is in your best interests. Remember
that a path followed by another is that person's
path—not your path.

Let yourself be guided by that which is within
you, that which is at one with everything and
therefore always knows the correct action and
the correct time to take that action. Using the *I
Ching* to discover answers to questions
concerning the right action at the right time is
one of the very best uses of the *I Ching*.

As you move along your path, it is a good idea
to occasionally check to see whether your

timing is right and that your actions are in accord with your highest and best good.

In *I Ching Wisdom* it states:

> *In following*
> *the path of the superior person,*
> *slight digressions from the good*
> *cannot be avoided,*
> *but*
> *you must turn back,*
> *before going too far.*

wu wei's comment:

Having turned onto the path of the inferior person, it is only natural that you will feel remorse, powerful remorse, but this is a good sign. However, you must not carry remorse too far; after making whatever amends you must, continue on, having resolved to be more cautious. To follow the path of the superior person takes great courage, firm determination, and fierce perseverance. You must watch like a hungry hawk for transgressions, and

22

finding them, you must turn back. This is an act of self-mastery, and highly commendable. Having turned back, you will progress like a hurricane, sweeping all obstacles from your path, and supreme good fortune and great success will quickly follow.

CHAPTER FIVE

LIVING THE *I CHING* LIFE

To awake in the morning and take a moment to refresh ourselves with the knowledge that we are divine beings in a sparkling Universe, to communicate with that sparkling Universe as though it were a dear friend, that is the start of an *I Ching* day. "Good morning," says the aware being, addressing All-That-Is, and, if it is appropriate, "Thank you for that most wonderful sleep."

At the heart of living life according to the wisdom of the *I Ching* is our knowledge that the Universe is alive and aware—aware of itself and aware of us. It may seem strange at first to communicate aloud or silently with All-That-Is, but as you become more and more aware that you are being heard, that there is communication going on in both directions, you will come to cherish the gift.

I capitalize "Universe" for the same reason I capitalize "God" because, for me, they are one and the same.

Keep aware as you read or listen to this book that you are living inside of, and are an inseparable part of, an alive, aware organism.

In *I Ching Wisdom* it states:

> *The superior person*
> *is reverent;*
> *at all times*
> *acknowledging the great Creator*
> *and the wonderousness*
> *of the universe.*

wu wei's comment:

When we see a great painting, we acknowledge the painter. When we see a great structure, we acknowledge the builder. When we see the Universe, the tiny portion of it that is visible to us, how can we fail to acknowledge its creator? When great grief or misfortune or illness befalls us, and no human can help, we instinctively turn to the divine for help; that is only natural, since each of us inherently knows the truth of his existence and origin. None of us can fathom how this universe of ours began, nor can any of us foretell when it will end. Not one of us can even say why it, or we, exist. Since we can only wonder at it all, does it not seem immensely egotistical and foolish not to be reverent in the face of that awesomeness?

Do you take your existence for granted without questioning that you are alive—that you have awareness? The major difference between humans and other life forms on our planet is our ability to reason and to question. Do you question the reason for your existence?

A friend of mine, a physicist who lives in Los Angeles, California, believes that there is no reason for our presence here on earth. He says, "We are just here." When I questioned him about his belief he said: "There has been enough time for us to evolve into who and what we are without the intervention of any supreme intelligence. There is no discernible cause beyond natural evolution, nor does there appear to be any reason for our existence, nor does there need to be. Since I have not been able to perceive any Divine Being or see any evidence that a Divine Being exists, or has ever existed, and since I only believe in what I can prove or at least see evidence of, I choose to believe that our existence is simply a matter of evolution and our awareness is simply a product of a complex biological organism."

Is that what you believe? That we, who are this wonderful life form, who can feel joy, love compassion, happiness, sadness, fear, wonder, who can create music and write poetry, who can appreciate beauty, that we are a product of an unthinking, unknowing, unaware, dead Universe? Are we to believe that the Universe of which we are a part and from whose substance we are made, which has produced us, is dead, yet we are alive? Are we so egotistical as to believe that we alone have awareness and intelligence and the rest of the Universe has not? Or are we to believe that we *are* the Universe, a portion of it, and that because we have intelligence and awareness, that it necessarily follows that the rest of the Universe also has intelligence and awareness, and in unimaginable abundance?

Do you believe in God or in a supreme being whom you call by another name, and, if so, do you believe that God is separate from you? My son, Pax, tells me that our very use of the word, "God," immediately implies separation, that those who use the word "God" are saying that they are separate from God, that they are not part of that supreme being to whom they are referring, that they are, in effect, disconnected.

To believe that we are simply a result, one of many, of a mindless universe where chaos reigns and we are but a chance manifestation is too lackluster for me, too empty. There is no wonder or magic in it. Neither is there any dignity or grandeur in that concept. To believe in a mindless, chaotic universe, necessarily means that we believe that the future is completely uncertain, that the Universe could end at any moment, that our existence is in the hands of chaotic, blind chance.

If chaos were the pervading condition, and chance ruled, the Universe could not continue, would not have continued, for all these trillions of years. If every moment, the continuation or discontinuation of existence were a chance occurrence, a moment-by-moment flip of the coin, and if heads meant to continue and tails meant to discontinue, to end it all, certainly by now, tails would have come up at least once, ending it long ago. That the Universe persists absolutely rules out, for me, the possibility that chaos reigns, that chance is the underlying condition of all of existence.

Chance and chaos seem to exist to those who believe in them only because they do not have enough of an overview to be able to perceive the order within which everything exists.

If you can, just for a moment, deliberately free your mind from what you have been told about religion, evolution, birth, death, and God, and any other concepts you have about why you're here on earth. Think clearly, on your own, about what you know of life and the world around you. Now, if you had to tell someone what you believed about the Universe and who we are and why we're here, just from your own personal observations, not repeating anything that anyone else has told you about God or religion, what would you tell that person? What do you make of it all?

The truth is that the closest any of us can come to a true religious experience on this planet is just being who we are at any moment. Being who we are is a pure religious experience. If we can stay with that experience, just being a part of All-That-Is, that's enough. We go searching, chasing after masters, because most of us want more than we have just being ourselves. If you want more, ask the person who knows what everything knows: yourself. Use the *I Ching* to ask, "Who am I in the Universal scheme of things?" "What happens when I die?" "Is there a life after death?" What is my mission on earth?" "What do I need to know about God?"

You do not have to seek immortality; you already have it. You are the Universe—just as much as anything in the Universe is the Universe.

All religions believe that a Deity, a God, a Supreme Being, by whatever name they choose to call "It," existed at the beginning of creation, and that everything that was created was created by and of the substance of that Supreme Being. For instance, most versions of the Bible of the Christian religion generally state that in the beginning there was only God. The Bible then goes on to say that God created the earth and the heavens. Since all there was in the beginning was God, according to the

Bible, it necessarily follows that everything that He created was created from Himself. If the religions are correct, it necessarily follows that everything in the Universe is alive and aware, saturated with the power, intelligence, and awareness of that great being from whom it was formed.

We may not be able to perceive life in a stone, but that does not mean that the stone does not live, does not have awareness. Crystal grows, rocks crumble into dust to be taken up and used by vegetables, which are, in their turn, eaten by animals, including ourselves, and when we and the other animals and the vegetables die, our bodies disintegrate and are taken up to be used by yet other life forms—an endless cycle, all alive, all aware.

If we were to peer into the heart of a stone at the atomic level, we would not see a dead, inert mass of material, but a furiously whirling mini-cosmos, much like what we see when we look into the night sky, but with its bits and pieces whirling at speeds near that of light.

There was a time when scientists were searching for the basic building blocks of the universe. First, they thought the smallest building blocks were molecules, then atoms; then, when they were able to peer into the heart of the atom, they discovered even smaller bits and pieces: neutrons, protons, a nucleus, then the even smaller quarks, gluons and neutrinos. The smaller particles have not yet been seen for they are too tiny and travel at furious speeds. We know of their existence only because of their footprints, the tracks they leave behind in their speeding whirl. It is their very speed that renders matter "hard." Just as when you look at a spinning airplane propeller, which appears to be an almost solid disk, so the whirling of the tiny particles creates the illusion of the hardness of matter. In reality, the same distance exists between the particles in an atom, relative to their size, as exists between the stars.

To appreciate the size of an atom, imagine a basketball as big as the earth, almost 8,000 miles in diameter. Next, imagine a golf ball, whirling around inside the earth-sized basketball. That is the relative size of an atom. To be able to appreciate the size of the nucleus within the atom, imagine that the golf ball is enlarged until its diameter is half a mile across. Now put a marble inside. That's the relative size of the nucleus inside an atom, and the nucleus itself is huge in comparison to the smaller particles.

Scientists have now discovered that the smallest of the particles appear and disappear, being formed from and dissolving back into seemingly empty space. However, space is not actually empty, nor is it really even space; it only appears as space because we can't see the energy which makes up space, which *is* space. It is this invisible field of energy from which matter is formed. Think of it—matter being created from space—an ocean of energy that intensifies, bringing "things" into being—energy changing from its primal form into another form, a physical form. The earth, the planets, the stars, other galaxies, ourselves, all are created from the same energy. Simply stated, energy and matter are one; therefore: all is one.

One day, when we have advanced far enough along our spiritual paths to be entrusted with the care of other parts of the Universe, we will be able to travel in the energy field, instantly being anywhere in the Universe we choose to be.

The creation of matter from energy is the desire of the Universe to manifest itself—to manifest itself in all its myriad forms. And we? We are the Universe experiencing itself. We, and all else that has been manifested from the energy field, are how the Universe experiences itself.

You might well ask: "How does this information affect us, and how can we use the information to lead better, fuller, more aware lives?" Once we perceive that our Universe is alive, a living, pulsating organism that has awareness and intelligence, vast intelligence, we come to know that the Universe and everything in it reacts to stimulation—our stimulation.

Just as we are stimulated by manifestations of the Universe such as weather changes and planetary and stellar influences, we also stimulate the Universe with our mood changes, our thoughts, and our actions. By being the way we are at every moment, we continually exert an influence on everyone and everything around us.

If you would for a moment, imagine a man who was angry all the time. Can you see how he would influence everyone around him? Can you see that, in a short time, he would be friendless? He would suffer from the results of his anger.

In *I Ching Wisdom* it states:

> *The small-minded person*
> *is not ashamed of unkindness*
> *and does not shrink from injustice.*

wu wei's comment:

The inferior person is unconcerned with unfairness or unkindness. As a result of natural law, he suffers, and he does not know that he is the cause of his suffering. The superior person feels diminished by acts of unkindness or injustice, whether committed by himself or another. As a result of natural law, he enjoys a life of great good fortune and contentment.

The above saying is one of many that shows how the Universe responds to our thoughts and actions.

By learning the laws of the Universe that are embodied in the *I Ching,* and by learning to live in harmony with those laws, what the *I Ching* describes as "living the life of the superior person, "we will eventually come to live in a manner that brings us peaceful harmony, long-lasting good fortune, great success and happiness—beings forever resonating with the great harmony. We will learn to flow with the ever changing events around us, smoothly integrating our actions into the Universal scheme. Anger, frustration, and despair will disappear, and feelings of well-being and exhilaration will pervade us as we experience sublime success.

Sublime success is more than just great success; it is the epitome of success and brings with it happiness, peace and spiritual wholeness. Success without happiness, peace, and spiritual wholeness is worthless. It is better to be unsuccessful and happy than successful and miserable.

Living life according to *I Ching* precepts permits us to avoid the pitfalls that beset the path of those who never give a thought to the consequences of their thoughts, words, or actions.

The *I Ching* asks, "If you are not as you should be, can anything happen except that you fall into a pit of your own creation?" Elsewhere in the great book it is stated, "Even the best opportunity in the hands of the wrong person comes to nothing."

Living the *I Ching* life means that we live according to what we know of the Universal laws and the ways they affect us.

In *I Ching Wisdom* it states:

> *Mad pursuit of pleasure*
> *never*
> *takes one to the goal.*

wu wei's comment:

No matter what your goal is, if you examine your motive in choosing the goal, you will discover that you have chosen it because you believe that it will bring you happiness. Those who seek their happiness in the mad pursuit of pleasure experience only temporary sensory enjoyment; they never arrive at the goal. Following the path of the superior person produces happiness, leads to happiness, and maintains happiness: deep down, soul-drenching happiness.

Lastly, we should be careful with whom we associate. Good friends are a great treasure, poor friends are a great detriment. Sometimes, when we are intent on reaching a goal, we associate with people with whom it is necessary for us to associate in order to reach our goal. At those times we should not let ourselves be enticed from the path of the superior person.

In *I Ching Wisdom* it states:

> *The superior person*
> *is never led into baseness*
> *or vulgarity*
> *by community of interests*
> *with people of low character.*

wu wei's comment:

We sometimes find ourselves associating with inferior people because of the need to achieve a common goal. In their company we may be tempted to pleasures and actions that are inappropriate for the superior person. To participate in such low pleasures or actions would certainly bring remorse. Just as we should not allow ourselves to be unresistingly swept along by unfavorable circumstances, neither should we allow inferior people to erode our good character. By our determination to continue in what we know to be right, we will overcome even the greatest of adversities, and success and good fortune are sure to be ours.

Use the *I Ching* to ask about a new friend. "What can I expect from entering into a relationship with my new friend?"

Being in the company of a well-intentioned friend has a wonderfully beneficial effect upon us, particularly if we take advantage of the opportunity to improve ourselves.

In *I Ching Wisdom* it states:

> If you see good,
> imitate it.
> If you have faults,
> rid yourself of them.

wu wei's comment:

This ethical attitude is the most important character attribute you can cultivate; it will lead to great good fortune and success. It is one of the ways the superior person further brightens his already bright virtue. For persevering in this effort, even among those considered lucky, you will stand out as the chosen one.

What we believe determines our actions. Our actions determine our future. The choice of how we live and what becomes of us is in our own hands.

CHAPTER SIX

CAUSE AND EFFECT

In our Universe, the law of cause and effect is absolute. Stated, the law says: "Every action produces a result, and the result is always in perfect accord with the action."

We may not know what results we will produce for taking certain actions. Through the use of the yarrow stalks and the *I Ching,* we can discover what actions to take that will produce results consistent with our highest and best good, what actions to avoid that will create pitfalls and disharmony for ourselves, and, if we have a specific action in mind, what will result from the taking of that action.

One of the most powerful effects in our lives is created as a result of who and what we believe ourselves to be. The moment our brains became functional, we began to build an image of who and what we believe ourselves to be.

All the events of our lives have helped to create that image. It is, "Who We Think We Are." Whenever we speak, act, and think, "Who We Think We Are," determines what the words, actions, and thoughts will be. We continually project "Who We Think We Are." Whenever we meet someone or walk into a room or consider the taking on of a new project, "Who We Think We Are" is who introduces himself and who walks into the room and who considers the new project. "Who We Think We Are" determines how we stand, whether we hold ourselves proudly erect or if we slouch. "Who We Think We Are" is our self image. It is who we believe ourselves to be.

If we know ourselves to be untruthful, cowardly, unfair, clumsy, a poor public speaker, weak-willed or any number of other poor characteristics, that's the image we hold in our minds and the image we project. It is the image that forms the basis for all the decisions we make in life. Similarly, if we know ourselves to be honorable, strong, brave, fair-minded, generous, clear-headed, articulate, or any number of other good characteristics, that's the image we project, and it also is the basis upon which we make our decisions. It's the law of cause and effect, and it brings in its trail all that goes with it, good and bad alike.

Our concept of "Who We Think We Are" changes as we change. By taking on the characteristics of the superior person, characteristics which are clearly defined within this book, we will come to see ourselves in a new light. Old images that existed in our minds of "Who We Think We Are" that have held us in place and prevented us from getting ahead will fall away, to be replaced by new images that will speed us successfully toward our goals. New characteristics will develop within us that will bring us great good fortune and sublime success. Remember, the rest of the Universe is *required* to respond to us as we are being at every moment.

Use the *I Ching* to ask, "How can I build good character?"   "What area of myself needs improvement?"

In *I Ching Wisdom* it states:

> *It is better to go on foot*
> *than ride in a carriage*
> *under false pretenses.*

wu wei's comment:

It is better to go honorably on foot and do without than to ride in a fine carriage under false pretenses and thereby lose your honor. If you pretend abundance when in fact you are in need, those who would aid you will not, either by believing you to be abundant or by recognizing your pretense and considering you to be unworthy. Furthermore, by pretending you have something when you do not, you diminish yourself in your own eyes and so lose self-respect.

Self respect is a product of "Who We Think We Are" The way we treat others is still another aspect of cause and effect.

In *I Ching Wisdom* it states:

> *Pleasant manners succeed*
> *even with irritable people.*

wu wei's comment:

> If we do not allow the irritability of others
> to affect our own pleasant conduct, our
> pleasant conduct then influences them.

By treating others well, we cause others to treat us well in turn. We will gain the respect of others because of our thoughtfulness and courtesy. Learn to see yourself as a pleasant person, courteous and respectful. Again, use the *I Ching* to ask, "What aspects of myself do I need to improve?"

Physics deals with the world of matter and energy. The law of cause and effect as it applies to physics says: "For every action there is an equal and opposite reaction." Metaphysics deals with the world beyond the physical. The law of cause and effect as it applies to metaphysics says: "For every action there is a response, and the response is in perfect accord with the action." If you plant an acorn, you get an oak tree, not a plum tree.

Knowing that actions produce effects in perfect accord with the actions allows you to produce any kind of effect that you desire. If you want to be popular, wealthy, healthy, loved, or anything else, determine what actions to take that will produce those effects. Use the *I Ching* to ask for guidance about what those actions should be. "What action should I take to improve my income this year?" How can I improve my relationship with my friends?" "What remedial action should I take to return to a state of health?" "What should I do to improve myself?"

As you progress through this book you will begin to take on more of the characteristics of a superior person, you will begin to see yourself in a new light. Natural law will do the rest.

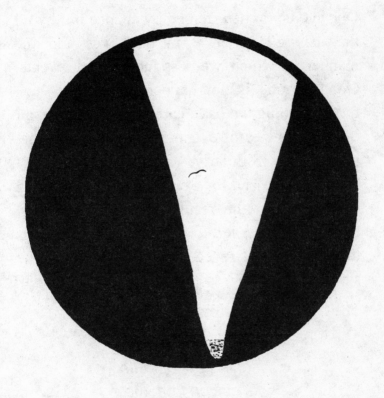

CHAPTER SEVEN

FATE

Our fate is not determined by chance but by all that has gone before in our lives and the manner in which we respond to new events. Good fortune is not happenstance good luck but something we have earned and is the result of a long series of events that have led to that moment. Similarly, ill fortune is not happenstance bad luck but a needed tap on the shoulder, also the result of a long series of events that have led to that moment, telling us that we have strayed from the path of the superior person.

The *I Ching* says of itself,

> *Neither far nor near,*
> *Neither dark nor deep,*
> *Is hidden from me.*

It sees into the heart of everything. Therefore,

we can use the *I Ching* to determine what actions to take that will be in our highest and best interests; to create our fate. We can actually bring about our own good fortune. We can ask anything so long as we ask sincerely and with reverence. In so doing, we soon come to discover that our higher consciousness is an unerring guide, a tool with which we can create our future.

After we have used our higher consciousness to gain answers, we should then ponder the answers to discover their subtleties. By following the guidance we have received and by acting in accord with that which is highest and best within us, we will, as a result of natural law, achieve supreme success and experience only sublime good fortune. That is how we create our fate.

The universe has many facets, from terrifying to playful, from destructive to nurturing. *Kua* 51, CHEN, is Shock, The Arousing. It is the trigram of CHEN, doubled, and it means the person asking the question has received or will receive a powerful shock, either physical, mental, emotional, or financial. The shock is a gift of the Universe and usually brings fear and trembling in its wake. When All-That-Is manifests itself in its terrifying forms: storms, earthquakes, fires, hurricanes, tragedies, or other severe shocks, the wise person examines his life to see whether he is living in accord with the highest principles. He takes stock of himself and orders his life. Finding any faults, he resolves to be a better person. He does not ignore the "tap on the shoulder" sent to him by an aware, loving Universe of which he is a part.

Years ago, I was gathering rocks for my flower garden. I had climbed about five feet into a forty-foot-deep ravine and was prying a rock of about 150 pounds from the top edge when my feet slipped from under me and I slid the remaining 35 feet to the bottom. The rock, which I had pried loose, was rolling down the steep slope after me. It landed on my head, opening a three-inch gash. The force of the blow drove me to the ground with such force that two bones in my hand were broken and welts were raised on my knees. I was afraid to reach up and feel my head because I thought I might feel my brain through the hole that I imagined must be there. That I was not knocked unconscious was an important part of what happened. As I lay in the mud, amazed that I was still alive and even more amazed that I had not lost consciousness, I wondered what good thing would come to me as a result of the blow to my head. As it turned out, my keeping aware that the blow to my head was for my benefit, was a key ingredient of the experience.

I went home and stood under a trickle of water from the shower and cleansed the wound. Later that day, I went to the doctor's office and had the wound stitched. Two weeks later, I did an *I Ching* reading to find out what my getting hit on the head was all about and received as an answer, *kua* 51, Chen, Shock, The Arousing.

The text read: "A manifestation of God. Shock brings success. It terrifies for a hundred miles, but the person who receives the shock does not let fall the sacrificial spoon and chalice." According to the text, I had received a shock which was a gift of God, and, in the midst of experiencing the shock, I had kept my awareness that the shock was a gift and that it was for my benefit. I wondered what the benefit was.

Several weeks later, I did an *I Ching* reading and discovered what the gift was: the blow to my head had opened channels in my brain that permitted clearer communication with my higher consciousness in conjunction with *I Ching*. Passages in the *I Ching* that had long been obscure to me became clear; the answers to new readings were as clear as though I were talking with a wise grandfather who knew all things and had my absolute good at heart. What a treasure for me! I would have gladly suffered the blow many times over to gain that precious gift, for with it, I am now able to better create a more favorable fate for myself and to walk more harmoniously with All-That-Is.

Anytime anything happens to you that seems unfortunate, even if it is hurtful or takes something precious from you, see it in the light of a beneficial occurrence. It may not be immediately apparent what the benefit is, but by treating the event *as though* it occurred for your benefit, you will preserve your good feelings, and by acting in accord with those good feelings you will, as a direct result of cause and effect, bring about a happy result.

Sometimes, if we don't discover on our own that we have strayed from the path of the superior person, it takes a shock to wake us up. Our job is to be grateful for the shock, to recognize it for the signpost it is, and to set our feet once more upon the path of good fortune. Failing that, we will most likely incur other shocks. The Universe has an endless supply of shocks it can deliver. In the Universe, there is no such thing as "reaching the bottom."

The Universe in which we live is inclined in our favor. That is also to say that it is inclined in its own favor since we and it are one. That the Universe is beneficially inclined is how and why it persists. Were it not that way, everything would have self-destructed long ago. An alive and aware Universe will not destroy itself.

That the Universe is favorably inclined can be seen in the numerical results of the yarrow stalk divination. The chances of getting a six, which is a dark, weak, unvirtuous, unbeneficial, broken line, are one in sixteen. The chances of getting a nine, which is a strong, light-giving, virtuous, beneficial, unbroken line, are three in sixteen. Therefore, the chances of getting a beneficial nine are three times greater than getting an unbeneficial six.

I strongly recommend the ancient use of yarrow stalks in divination rather than the modern coin method because the three coins, being limited to heads or tails, do not have sufficient mathematical possibilities to adequately represent the continual unfolding of the Universe. The forty-nine yarrow stalks do possess sufficient mathematical possibilities. (You can read a full discussion of the yarrow stalk method versus the coin method in *The I Ching,* also published by Power Press, Los Angeles, California. Yarrow stalks can also be obtained from your local book store or from Power Press.)

After using the *I Ching* for only a short while, we see clearly that our fate is in our own hands, and that, while we may have heretofore created our future unknowingly and with sorrowful results, we can now create it knowingly and with joyous results.

In *I Ching Wisdom* it states:

*The way of the superior person
is to be joyous of heart,
yet concerned in thought.*

wu wei's comment:

> The superior person is concerned in
> thought because he knows that all
> periods of prosperity are followed by
> times of decline and all people are not as
> they should be. He therefore takes
> thought for the future and exercises
> caution in his dealings with people.
> Nonetheless, no matter how concerned
> he is in thought, nor how weighty those
> thoughts may be, his concerns are never
> enough to dim his inner joy because,
> above all, he remains aware that he is an
> indestructible child of a golden Universe.

As you travel along your path toward
enlightenment, keep a joyous outlook on life.
Keep aware that you are an indestructible child
of a golden Universe.

It will be of enormous benefit to you in

creating your fate to understand that you are truly eternal, that you are here forever. The major argument in favor of reincarnation is that we are here now.

Perhaps your life has not been very enjoyable this time around and you don't want to come back. That's understandable, but you are a Universal life form, come to earth to perfect yourself as a divine incarnation, and perfect yourself you must. Read the top half of Chapter One again.

In determining what you fate will be, it is well to keep in mind that as you traverse your path to enlightenment, you will encounter many obstacles. Knowing in what light to see those obstacles will be of great benefit. First, the obstacles are there completely for your benefit; second, the obstacles are there as signposts telling you that you are slightly or greatly off course; third, the obstacle is a workout situation designed to strengthen certain areas within you that need strengthening. Looking at obstacles in that light will cause you to respond to them differently from the way you now respond. Remember that even the worst thing that can happen to you will be of great benefit you.

In *I Ching Wisdom* it states:

> *Only a person*
> *who goes to meet his fate*
> *resolutely*
> *will be equipped*
> *to deal with it*
> *adequately.*

wu wei's comment:

To meet fate resolutely means that you have the determination to overcome whatever fate may bring, that you will not succumb to folly or temptation, and that you will not be turned aside from your chosen course. Only a strong or courageous person can stand up to his fate, overcoming all obstacles. His fierce determination enables him to endure to the end. This strength or courage shows itself in facing things exactly as they are, without any sort of self-deception or illusion. It is then that a light develops out of events by which the path to success may be recognized. By making this strong commitment, you actually cause favorable events to occur that would otherwise not have occurred. A person capable of this kind of commitment can reach any goal.

Keep aware of who and what you are as you become involved in the affairs of the world. You are an indestructible child of a golden Universe. Remember, the greatest deed, the creation of the Universe, has already been done. In the face of that , all else is possible.

CHAPTER EIGHT

RELATIONSHIPS

A relationship is like a garden. To create a condition that will cause our plants to thrive and produce abundantly, we must weed, water, fertilize, communicate with, and care for the plants in our garden. We must also know about the special needs of the plants we're caring for. Some need more or less light than others; some need special fertilizers; some need more or less water than others. To create a wonderful, long-lasting, fruitful relationship, we must create a favorable condition within which our relationship will thrive and endure and to do this we must know about the special needs of our partners.

Most importantly, to have our relationships last, we must cultivate the quality of endurance within ourselves.

In *Ching Wisdom* it states:

> *To enjoy a meaningful way of life,*
> *and to produce long-lasting effects,*
> *the ability to endure*
> *must be firmly established*
> *within you.*

wu wei's comment:

To endure means to continue in the face of obstacles, pain, fatigue, frustration, opposition, or hardship. To endure is to continue to the end. Duration is a state that is not worn down by anything. It seems almost needless to say that when we have established the quality of endurance within ourselves that we can reach any goal, overcome any obstacle, and bear any condition. Once established, this inner law of our being then determines all of our actions and leads to supreme good fortune and great success.

To achieve the goal of endurance, it is necessary for us to fix our minds on the goal of endurance, that our relationships will survive through the difficulties, failures, successes, and changes that all relationships encounter as part of the human condition.

Once we have committed ourselves to the goal of endurance, all decisions we make that affect our relationship will be made with that goal in mind, and our relationships will therefore endure as a process of natural law—cause and effect.

An example may assist in making clear what has been stated. Suppose you are in a love relationship and your mate has not learned or been taught to feel secure about relationships. Suppose there is a person with whom you are friendly and whose company you enjoy, but who causes your mate to feel insecure and jealous. What do you do? You explain the situation to your friend who is the object of your mate's jealousy, and, at least for awhile, put your relationship with that person on hold.

Once you have created the safe atmosphere within which your love relationship can thrive, you can then work on building a secure base for your partner so that you can enjoy relationships with others without having the insecure feeling of jealousy arise in your partner.

You may think to yourself, "If I have to stop seeing my friend because my mate is insecure, is the relationship worth it? Why does everything I do have to be to done in the light of my decision to protect and preserve the relationship?" The answer is that for relationships to endure, that kind of thoughtfulness and care are needed. Wouldn't you like to have someone care about you in that way?

SAFE ATMOSPHERE AND THE REAL YOU

Communication is probably the single most important aspect of creating an enduring relationship. To be able to communicate freely and productively, a condition must be created within which the communication can take freely take place. "Safe atmosphere" means that each of you can openly speak to the other without fear of incurring anger, criticism, or reprisal. If your partner tells you something in confidence, and a week later you use it against your partner, chances are, you will have destroyed the "safe atmosphere" and communication will become difficult if not impossible. Similarly, if your partner tells you something personal and you become angry, you have most likely destroyed the safe atmosphere wherein those types of confidences can be exchanged. You and your partner should set out some ground rules that will insure that each of you can freely and openly communicate thoughts and feelings to the other without fear of reprisal.

There are two main aspects of being able to communicate freely and productively. The first is that both partners must know who is "the real you." By that, I mean that both partners need to understand themselves and each other in the light of their past experiences. To achieve such understanding, each partner must communicate to the other all important experiences shared with all the other important relationships including parents or surrogate parents, close friends, and other love relationships.

Those relationships created impressions and behavior patterns that will carry over into the current relationship, affecting it in many ways. Because each of the partners has had different experiences, each partner will react differently to the ever unfolding events of the relationship. To be able to understand why a partner reacts to an event in the way that he or she does is critical to being able to cope with the reaction. An example will help to demonstrate the concept of "the real you."

Cory and Tiffany lived together for three years. Every Christmas, Thanksgiving, or vacation time, there was great dissension. The dissension was created by Tiffany who started fights on those occasions for no obvious reason, destroying the harmony of the holiday. Cory walked on eggshells to avoid dissension at holiday times, but no amount of caution could save the day from disaster. Tiffany was by far the stronger of the two personalities, being an aggressive, outgoing sales agent for an insurance company, while Cory was a quiet, unassertive computer programmer. Cory felt helpless and didn't know of any action he could take to remedy the situation. He asked Tiffany if she would go for counseling, but the suggestion only made her angry.

One day, Cory came to me and told me of the problem. I showed him how to do an *I Ching* reading, and he asked the question, "What can I do to help Tiffany solve her problem of ruining our holidays?" The answer he received was *kua* 18, Ku, Correcting Deficiencies. The ancient text talks about correcting deficiencies caused by the mother or the father. The bottom line of the *kua* was obtained with a six which meant that it was a moving line that held meaning for Cory. It states: "Correcting deficiencies caused by the father. You are in a weak position without much strength and will not receive any help, but the deficiency can be corrected by hard work. There is danger in the situation, so caution is required, but in the end, good fortune."

I suggested that Cory talk with Tiffany about the holidays she had shared with her parents. Because the *kua* said that Cory was in a weak position without much strength, and from what he had told me of Tiffany's anger when he brought up the subject, I suggested that he start the conversation by reminiscing with Tiffany about his own holiday times spent with his parents. That would create the safe atmosphere for Tiffany to talk about her own family holidays.

Tiffany's mother and father had gone through a messy divorce when Tiffany was four years old, and her mother remarried a year later. Her mother and stepfather moved several states away from her father, and Tiffany rarely saw her father after that.

Bolstered by the reading that said hard work was required but in the end good fortune would come, one evening, Cory talked with Tiffany about the times he had spent with his family at various holidays. After awhile, Tiffany commented that the holiday times she had spent with her mother and stepfather were filled with dissension and anger. Cory asked why that was, but Tiffany refused to talk about it and became somewhat distant.

The *kua* into which 18 transformed by virtue of the bottom moving line was 26, Ta C'hu, Great Restraint. Since Cory's question was about what he could do to help Tiffany, the text of *kua* 26 meant that Cory should strongly restrain himself in his responses to Tiffany regarding what she would tell him about her prior family history. Cory wisely did not press the issue, but a few days later began to talk again about the times he had spent with his parents during holidays. After awhile, Tiffany again offered the comment that the time she spent with her parents at holidays was a disaster. Cory only said "Oh?" suggestively, and the tale was finally told.

Tiffany's stepfather was a retired army man who saw himself as a tough guy, a hard taskmaster. He also had a sadistic nature. Immediately after he married Tiffany's mother, he began to mentally dominate four year old Tiffany. His favorite ploy to get Tiffany to do what he wanted was to create the illusion that something in the future was going to provide a wonderful surprise for Tiffany, such as "Wait until you see what I bought for you for Christmas! You're going to love it!" He would make that statement four or five months before Christmas. Then the next time he wanted Tiffany to do something she didn't want to do, he'd say, "If you don't do it, I won't give you your Christmas present." Thereafter, he would constantly use the threat of not giving her the present right up until Christmas morning when he would cause a nasty argument and, of course, there would be no present, no matter how good Tiffany had been. Her stepfather destroyed every Christmas day, and every time he blamed it on Tiffany, making it her fault.

Similarly, he would promise a wonderful vacation. He would talk for weeks about the vacation and all its wonders and the fun they would have. Then, when he wanted Tiffany to obey him, he would threaten her with the loss of the vacation. "If you don't do what I tell you to do, I won't take you on the vacation I told you about." He would keep that up until the day of the vacation and then, the morning they were to leave, he would cause an argument that would result in the loss of the vacation, always blaming the loss on Tiffany. The same scenario unfolded every

Thanksgiving, Fourth of July, Halloween, Easter and Labor Day weekend.

This torturous behavior kept up until Tiffany was about ten and she started to rebel. Her rebellion took the form of destroying the holidays before he could do it. She would not wait for him to ruin the holiday; she would do it herself, and quickly. In this way she protected herself from hurt and disappointment. It was that conditioning that she was bringing into her relationship with Cory.

The *kua* also said that Cory would benefit by helping Tiffany if he would assist her in her job (earning a living). To that effect he designed a computer program that greatly assisted her in keeping track of her clients. The *kua* also stated that he would be benefited if he undertook a major project. In accordance with that, he began to look into the purchase of a home for himself and Tiffany. The last part of the *kua* said that Cory would be benefited by talking to someone who had great experience in the field of psychology (studying the deeds of our ancient heroes and familiarizing himself with great sayings of antiquity). He went to see a psychologist and thoroughly acquainted himself with Tiffany's problem. Within a year, Tiffany and he shared wonderful holidays together, they lived in a new home, and Tiffany was earning more money, thanks to Cory's computer program.

No matter how often I do *I Ching* readings, I never fail to be amazed at the accuracy of the readings and the way the answers fit the questions so perfectly.

The decisions we make without a mate are oftentimes not the decisions we need to make as a partner in a relationship. It is not enough to say that we will treat our partners in the same fashion that we would like to be treated. Our partners may require care beyond that which we need. Everyone's needs are different, so, in nurturing a relationship, it is important for us to find out what the needs of our mates are and to provide for them. Very few relationships come to us exactly as we want them, but, with the proper care, we can shape them into enduring pillars of strength and beauty within which great joy can be experienced and great deeds can be accomplished.

A friend who was experiencing the ending of a relationship he had enjoyed for two years was lamenting to me that he was "a very bad chooser of women," that all the women he picked seemed to be flawed in some way or another, and that, in the end, the flaw caused the break-up of the relationship. He asked me, "Why do all the women I choose for relationships have fatal flaws?"

I told him that the women he chose did not have fatal flaws, that it was he who created the fatal flaws in his mates by his own behavior. I told him that we all have the full range of potential within ourselves to be either great and wonderful or mean and nasty, that it is we ourselves who bring out the good or bad qualities in our mates by being the way we are at every moment. It is in just that same way that our own good and bad qualities are brought out by the people with whom we have relationships.

INTEGRITY

Relationships require complete integrity. The first time we lie or are untrue to the person with whom we share a relationship, we condemn ourselves and our partner to a second class relationship. First class relationships are possible only when they exist in an atmosphere of total trust. If you are in a relationship and have already been less than completely truthful with your partner, you can remedy the fault by making your partner aware of your error and of your intention to be honorable in the future. Sometimes that type of remedial action results in the loss of the relationship, but it is better not to have the relationship than to maintain the relationship and exist in a condition of dishonor and distrust, sharing a relationship that is less than all it could be.

I know a man who had been unfaithful to his mate. I suggested to him that he be truthful with her and tell her of his infidelity. His comment to me was: "She couldn't handle the truth." The fact is, he's the one who can't handle the truth. He's afraid of the consequences of the truth. He's afraid she'll leave him if she finds out he's been unfaithful to her. So, they are now forced to live a lie, existing in a relationship in which there is no trust.

In *I Ching Wisdom* it states:

> *The superior person*
> *is completely sincere·*
> *in his thoughts and actions.*

wu wei's comment:

In sorrow and reverence, your feeling must mean more to you than ceremoniousness, which is primarily for the benefit of others. In personal expenditures, you must place the highest value on thrift. In conduct, your actions should be simple and unpretentious. Neither should you pretend love or other emotions that you do not feel; like all false illusions, they only bring hurt and despair in their train and bode ill for the pretender. There is no need to pretend or deceive; fix your eyes on the path of the superior person, be yourself, and all else will be accomplished as a result of natural law.

Using the *I Ching* to maintain a relationship is wonderfully effective. You can ask questions such as: "What can I do to strengthen my relationship?" "What should I be paying attention to now regarding my relationship?" "How will my relationship be affected if I take this new job that has been offered?" "What can I do to help my mate?"

If you want to begin a relationship with someone and don't know how to proceed, you can ask, "What can I do to have a relationship with John/Susan?" It is always important to ask, "What can I expect from this new relationship?"

Maintain your individuality and take responsibility for yourself. Do not make the mistake of relying completely on your relationships for your happiness.

In *Ching Wisdom* it states:

> *If you depend on your relationships*
> *for your happiness,*
> *you will either be happy or sad*
> *as your relationships*
> *rise and fall.*

wu wei's comment:

That is the fate of those who depend on others for their happiness. To avoid such a fate, wed your happiness to that which endures: the path of the superior person. A quiet, self-contained joy, desiring nothing from without, and resting content

> with everything, remains independent and
> free, and in this freedom lies good fortune
> because it harbors the quiet security of a
> heart fortified within itself.

Therefore, while you should take the best care possible of your relationships, remember that you came into this world alone, and you shall depart from it alone. In the meantime, do not burden your relationships with the task of making you happy. Make yourself happy with the quality of your thoughts and what you know of the Universe and the way it works. When you have accomplished that goal, you will be able to make your partner happy because your partner will be in the company of a happy person.

In *I Ching Wisdom* it states:

> *In friendships*
> *and close relationships,*
> *you must make a careful choice.*

wu wei's comment:

Certain people uplift you; others pull you down. Certain people give you strength; others sap your energy. Choose carefully. Good friends, like good neighbors, are an endless benefit. Bad relationships can ruin a lifetime. Following the path of the superior person permits a natural selection that will find you only with the best quality friends.

The same applies to the selection of a mate.

In *I Ching Wisdom* it states:

In the time of gathering together,
make no arbitrary choice of your associates.
There are secret forces at work,
leading together
those who belong together.

wu wei's comment:

An arbitrary choice is one that is made on the basis of personal preference, without regard to laws or principles. In the time of gathering together, the secret forces that are leading together those who belong together may bring people who are not of your personal preference but who, nonetheless, will be of great benefit. The saying, therefore, counsels us in two ways: one, that we should remain open-minded, and two, that we need not have concerns about finding the right people.

If you are seeking a mate or partner, you need have no fear of not finding the right person. The Universe, which is aware of you, knows what and who you need for your growth. If indeed you are to have a partner in a relationship, exactly the right partner will be provided. What you make of the relationship once you have it, is entirely in your own hands.

In the selection of a mate or partner, be observant. There is an old saying that love is blind. In many ways that is a blessing because it helps us to be tolerant of our mates or partners. However, it is also important not to deceive ourselves about the person we're interested in.

In *I Ching Wisdom* it states:

> If we want to know what anyone is like,
> we have only to observe
> on what he bestows his care
> and what sides of his own nature
> he cultivates and nourishes.

wu wei's comment:

Each person reveals himself by what he says and does, by the way he dresses, by the ways he responds to events, by what he reads and watches, and generally, by the way he lives life. By observing anyone, we can see what that person is like.

The best way to build your relationship is to build your mate or partner.

CHAPTER NINE

INTEGRITY AND FEAR

Integrity is one of the single most important character traits we can develop. Integrity extends far beyond the telling of truth. It has to do with how we perform our tasks, how we treat the people we come in contact with, how we respond to events and whether or not we can be trusted, and, in the end, our integrity or lack of it produces the quality of our lives.

Truthfulness is one aspect of integrity. What is it? All the truth, all the time. All lies have their basis in fear. The only reason we have ever lied was that we were afraid. All our fears were based upon our expectations of bad results. We knew what the truth was, but we believed that if we told it, we would experience a bad consequence. If we had expected a beneficial effect to result from our telling the truth, we would have done it. Instead, what we did was to re-shape what had happened or was going to happen, and then told it in a way that we hoped would trick our listeners into believing our improvised version of reality.

By doing that, did we change the reality of what happened? No, the truth still existed; it just distorted the situation and created something we then had to cope with.

Telling the truth brings us directness of mind. The waste of time and energy in planning, executing, and maintaining a lie is eliminated from our lives. We enjoy straight thinking and straight talking which takes us straight to our goals.

To experience fear, we are required to use our imaginations to project a bad outcome. We can just as easily use our imaginations to project a beneficial outcome. It may not always seem as if it's a choice, but it is. Where does the fear come from? Is it in the situation itself, or is it necessary for us to use our imaginations to create the fear? To find the answer, we can ask ourselves, "Who imagines the situation turning out badly?"

Fear and courage go hand in hand. To face our fears takes courage, but we all have that. How much? As much as is necessary to face the greatest fear we can possibly experience. For being courageous and acting truthfully in the face of our fears, we not only experience a beneficial outcome; we also gain strength and improve our self image; we get to feel really good about ourselves.

Fear can block us unless we call forth our courage, which then empowers us to act.

All experiences that cause us to feel fear are directed at our weakest areas. The experience comes to us so we can use our courage to overcome the fear, thereby strengthening our weak area. These workout situations are completely for our benefit, and, for seeing them through courageously, we not only strengthen ourselves, we also gain a bonus benefit as well. The bonus benefit is a gift for having passed the test and is different each time.

In *I Ching Wisdom* it states:

> *To remain at the mercy*
> *of moods*
> *of hope and fear*
> *will cost you*
> *your inner composure and consistency.*

wu wei's comment:

Hope contains the subtle fear that what we hope for will not come to pass. Fear contains the subtle hope that what we fear will not come to pass. Neither state is appropriate to the superior person who turns everything to his advantage, and who therefore knows that everything that occurs is for his benefit. To remain at the mercy of hope and fear is to bob like a cork on the ocean, rising and falling as our hopes and fears assail us. Living the life of the superior person is certain to secure our fates and bring us supreme success and good fortune. Therefore, we should all have courage and faith, we should all be joyous, and all will be well. We are far more powerful than we suspect, and the universal plan includes our well being.

The *I Ching* is of immense value in overcoming fear and exposing the truth. I use the term, "exposing the truth," to indicate that whenever the cause of our fear is unmasked, there is the shining kernel of truth informing us that there is nothing that can happen to us that will not be to our great benefit, even the worst thing that can happen.

Using the *I Ching*, you can ask, "What do I need to know about my current fear?" "What will happen if my current fear materializes? "What can I do to eliminate the cause of my fear?

People have asked me, "What about the people who have AIDS or cancer or Alzheimer's who will die a painful, demoralizing death? Shouldn't they be afraid? What benefit could they possibly derive from those horrible diseases?" Those are truly difficult situations to see as being beneficial, but remember Chapter One: "That intelligent, creative, aware force (that created and sustains us) endlessly shapes and alters us, changes us, to the purpose that we will ultimately come to achieve our true nature."

The ancient Chinese sage who stated that so many thousands of years ago knew that the Universe was favorably inclined, and he perceived then those same truths that are available to us now: "Change is constant," and "Every event benefits us."

Just when we are beginning to understand that everything that befalls us benefits us, it may be difficult to perceive the benefits that come to us through a major catastrophe or a great illness. It is better to start with small things, like a stubbed toe, and see whether we can find a benefit in that, perhaps by trying to believe that the stubbing of our toe released an acupressure point, and being thankful for the experience.

When a seemingly unfortunate event befalls us, it may not always be immediately clear to us what the benefit is, but responding to the event or circumstance as though it were for our benefit is the magical formula that will keep us in harmony with the ever unfolding Universe. Use the *I Ching* to ask: "What is the benefit for me in the calamity I have just experienced?" If you feel fear, ask: "What benefit will I receive if I face my fear?"

Whenever something happens that is unpleasant, or seems unlucky, our job is to say, "That was for my benefit." Then, by responding as though what happened was for our benefit, we cause the law of cause and effect to bring about the desired end.

Experiencing fear can have a beneficial effect. Fear can provide us with the same benefit that danger provides: it is a warning. It means that we should take action to correct the situation that is causing our fear.

Remember that losing your integrity by succumbing to your fear is a poor trade-off. It helps to imagine yourself as the hero in a story. Imagine how you would want your hero to act in the situation you're faced with, imagine the rewards your hero will get for acting courageously, and then as act as you would want your hero to act.

CHAPTER TEN

THE GOD GAME

When I was a brash youngster, I sat one evening in front of my fire wondering what it would be like to be God; the popular conception of God: all powerful, all-seeing, and all-knowing. My first thought was, "How boring! There's nobody to talk to, at least not on God's level, and what's there to talk about anyway, when everything is known, past, present and future? There's nothing to do God hasn't done, nothing to see God hasn't seen, and nothing to know God doesn't already know. Imagining myself as God, I saw that the situation I imagined was intolerable, so, as God, I created a game for myself to play, "The God Game."

I began to think about what the game would be like, what it would *have* to be like for me to be able play. The two main problems were my omniscience, (my all-knowingness) and the need for a game board on which to play. I solved both of those problems with one stroke: I created the Universe. Instead of playing *on* the board, I would play *in* the board.

Since I was all that existed, I had to create the Universe from myself. (The Latin derivative of "universe" is "unus" meaning "one," and "versus," meaning, "to turn into." In this case, One, turned into the Universe.) To create the new Me, the Universe, I spread my energy out into infinity, willing it to create. To create what? Well, look around; that's what I created: All-That-Is.

Every particle of the new Universe was created from my energy field and was saturated with my God-Beingness, my God-Power, my God-Awareness, and my God-Creativity. *Every* particle. And, wonder of wonders, every manifested particle was different from every other manifested particle.

In the creation of the Universe, I had used up all of Me. There was no little box somewhere with leftover mountain ranges, skies, galaxies, stars or planets. Everything was used up—and it was in its exact right place. It still is. We cannot be out of place in the Universe. Wherever we are, that's where we're supposed to be, doing whatever it is that we're doing.

Whether what we are doing will bring us good fortune or ill fortune depends on what we are doing and our intention in doing it, whether we intend good or evil.

The other major problem, the one about my omniscience, my all-knowingness and all-seeingness, was solved by my having turned myself into all those little bits and pieces of the Universe. My God awareness/knowledge/power/creativity was spread out over the totality, each little particle receiving its share, and my omniscience was lost.

Of course, I couldn't abandon my powers

without a set of rules by which to play. That would leave everything in the hands of blind chance, what people today call "chaos." If I did that and something went wrong, there would just be oblivion, as when the lights go out, and because I was/am eternal, as is my Universe, the lights would be out forever.

So into being came: The Laws Of The Universe. Because I wanted to keep the game interesting, the first Law was that of Change. That Law decrees that All-That-Is will be in a state of constant change—everything except the Laws; they will remain eternally unchanging.

The next law was that of Cause and Effect. That Law provided for a response to every action and that the response would be in perfect accord with the action.

I created the Law of Conservation Of Energy, which decrees that none of the energy in my newly created Universe, from which All-That-

Is was formed, could be lost or damaged, only changed. That's because everything that exists is made from Me, *is* Me, and I didn't want to lose any of Me.

I made many Physical Laws, laws that would govern matter, such as the Law of Gravity that attracts physical things. That Law provides that matter contains gravity; doubling the mass of matter, doubles the gravity.

I created the Law of Evolution. That Law provides for the development of organisms along lines that lead toward ever greater complexity and consciousness. Eventually, after trillions of years, that Law brought forth Thinking Beings, each one gifted with a tiny portion of all my original God Powers: the power to imagine, to do, to create, and to destroy. Not to destroy in the total sense of the word (I left that power out), but to destroy in the sense that killing would return a portion of All-That-Is to its original energy state, such as when paper burns and releases itself as heat energy and is absorbed back into the mass of total energy.

Of course, the game had to have an object, a way to win. So what was the object of the game? For all Thinking Beings to become aware of Who They Are. When enough of us became aware of Who We Are, we would reach a point of critical mass, when everyone would instantly become aware of Who They Are, and the game would be won.

I wanted us to know when we were on the path to winning and losing the game, so I created pain and joy. Whenever we would feel happiness or joy, we'd be on the path to winning; when we'd feel unhappiness, frustration, or pain, we'd be on the path toward losing. Since I had created eternity within which to play, I tipped the scales toward winning because to never win through all eternity would be like losing, and I didn't want to lose.

When I had scattered my total knowledge and I had a place to play and rules by which to play, the game was on, and I could play. Welcome to the game.

CHAPTER ELEVEN

TIME, ETERNITY AND US

In *I Ching Wisdom* it states:

> *The superior person*
> *sees*
> *and understands*
> *the transitory*
> *in the light of eternity.*

wu wei's comment:

We imagine an endless future stretching out ahead of us and an endless past stretching out behind. We believe that where we exist is the moment we call "now," the moment we believe to be a tiny hairline that separates the future from the past. The reverse is true; all there is and was and ever will be is an endless "now." Is it not always "now"? The superior person understands that this moment we call "now" is all that exists and, as such, is as much of eternity as eternity itself. He therefore understands that whatever occurs within this moment of "now," is perfect, just as eternity is perfect. Carrying his thought further, he understands that being part of eternity, he is perfect—and—you are perfect. Anyone who completely grasps that concept will feel his sense of impermanence evaporating as mist in the air.

To understand the transitory, that which passes away, see those things that pass away in the light that every ending contains a new beginning. However, even endings and beginnings are illusions. They are simply situations and matter flowing into different forms. Matter is transitory only in the sense that its form changes. Everything, in its essence, is eternal.

Being part of the Universe, we, too, are eternal. Whether when we die we keep our individuality and exist on another level, another dimension, or lose our individuality and merge into the totality of All-That-Is is of little consequence; either end is magnificent.

Time is one. It seems to flow onward, to progress, because we age and change occurs. Also, because we can't put two physical objects in the same space at the same time, we conceive of "before" and "after," all of which, our reason tells us, means that time flows on.

However, what our senses and our reason tell us about time is misleading: "before" and "after" exist within the totality of time. Time is the chalkboard on which "before" and "after" write themselves. To conceive of that more easily, imagine writing a sentence on a chalkboard. Does the board unfold as you write, creating more of itself as you write each letter? No. The total board exists all the time. It is the same with time; it exists completely, all at once, and within it, change takes place.

For us to be able to hear sound, there must be a silence within which the sound can be heard. For us to be able to perceive change, there must be a changelessness against which change can be seen. For us to be able to perceive movement, there must be non-movement against which the movement can be seen. With time also, there must be a "no-time," or an endless time; an "is-ness." "No-time" is the consciousness of the Universe, and it pervades everything. Within that consciousness, as part of that consciousness, we exist.

In *A Tale Of The I Ching*, *Fu Hsi* tells his disciple what the "Void" is, and he speaks of change. Their conversation follows.

Fu Hsi said, "It is time for you enter into the Void."

"The Void? Where is that?"

"That is what I call the space where everything exists before it is formed. It is as if you had an image in your mind of a figure, and then you carved the figure out of wood. Before the wooden figure emerged, the idea of it was in your thoughts. It is the same with everything that exists; an image of everything exists in the void before it is created, a perfect image. Do you know what a mold is?"

"Yes, Great Master. I have a shell into which I pack wet sand. Then I turn the shell upside down and tap it lightly, then I remove the shell. The sand remains formed in the image of the shell. The shell is a mold."

"Exactly."

The disciple opened his mouth to ask whether there was a mold for himself, but then he realized that Fu Hsi had just told him that everything had a mold, so he closed his mouth and withheld his question.

Fu Hsi, who seemed to miss nothing, smiled and said, "Yes, you too have a mold."

The disciple colored a bit but recovered quickly from his small embarrassment and said, "Revered Master, do the images from which all things come change?"

Fu Hsi smiled. "Are you asking that question because you have seen that everything is always changing?"

This time the disciple had to comment, "You always seem to be able to read my thoughts. Yes, that is why I ask."

"That is a good question. The answer is that the image is fully formed, including all of its states of change, from its birth to its seeming death, all at the same time."

When *Fu Hsi* told his disciple that the images of everything are completely formed, including all their states of change, he was saying that time is one, that everything exists within "no-time," or endless time. It is like a video tape of a movie. The entire movie is there on the video tape from its beginning to its end. To experience the movie, we must play the tape. We watch as the film unfolds, yet at all times, the entire film exists. It is that way with time. In the void exist the images of everything, including all their states of change.

Our sun will, at some time millions of years in the future, become a giant red star, expanding to many times its current size. It will engulf the earth, and our little planet will be returned to the void. Does that mean that the human race as we know it is doomed? Hardly that. But it does mean that we will necessarily go through some transitions.

Our existence on this planet is very frail. If, for instance, a deadly virus such as the AIDS virus were to be transmitted by air rather than by blood, it would quickly destroy human life. If we continue to heat the atmosphere, and the polar ice caps begin to melt, we will lose our dry land. If we continue to destroy the ozone layer with pollutants and the destruction of our greenery, radiation from the sun will eventually destroy us.

Is that the end for us? No, of course not. It only means that this most beautiful planet will, at some time in the future, become uninhabitable. As for us, we will either be reabsorbed into the totality of the Universe, or we will retain our individuality and appear in some other part of the Universe. As stated elsewhere in the book, either end is magnificent.

So, relax, be of good cheer. We are in the best of all possible hands: the hands of Universe. Remember, the Universe is here and everything is possible. A Universe capable of creating itself can do anything and everything.

I realize this chapter opens the possibility of endless discussions about fate, free will, and chaos, but this little book is not the place for those discussions. It is enough to know that we are eternal, that for walking the path of the superior person we will soar to great heights of good fortune and success, that the Universe is alive and aware, and that we are part of it all.

CHAPTER TWELVE

CHILDREN

"You're wonderful, and I love you." Fortunate indeed is the child whose parents say those wonderful, stabilizing words many times during his or her childhood years. To implant that message deeply in the psyche of our children is a gift almost beyond reckoning. Whenever misfortune or setbacks occur in the child's life, whenever criticism or rejection is encountered, there are those words, feeding the child from a deep level: "You're wonderful, and I love you."

Infants are spirits, divine beings who come to earth to gain experience. Our job as parents, educators, friends, or guardians is to provide the correct information to the children so that they will be able to act on the basis of what is true in the Universe rather than on superstition or false beliefs, and to provide the child with a good self image.

What we learn as children sets the pattern for the rest of our days on earth. We all begin as babies with unspoiled, fresh, pure minds, free from care, free from prejudice, free from thoughts of hate, anger, and fear. The chalkboards of our minds are clear, ready to be written upon by our parents, teachers, friends, experience, and ourselves. We are ready to learn.

Parents generally think of their children as "theirs" and believe that they have the right to do with them as they see fit. Some parents feel the child as a burden, an unwelcome obligation; others feel blessed. Fortunate is the child whose parents understand their true roles: teachers, guides, protectors, providers. Even more fortunate is the child whose parents understand that they and their child are spiritually connected, that their association goes back to the beginning of the Universe, that they have come here, to this planet, in advance of their child to pave the way, to lead their child into a correct understanding of the child's mission here on earth.

I know of no more important information that a child can receive than that the Universe is alive and aware, reacting to the child's every state of being, every thought, every action, and that the child is a part of that Universe, an inseparable, eternal part.

We may have forgotten how we came to earth, but however we got here, the circumstances were exactly right for each of us. That is vitally important for our children to know if they are to lead great lives. All developing souls require growth in particular areas of soul life, and the circumstances into which each of us is born provide perfectly for that growth.

It is not only useless for us to lament the circumstances into which we were born and the conditions under which we were raised; it is also detrimental to our growth as individuals and a sign of our unawareness. No matter the circumstances of our childhood, no matter the care or lack of it we received from our parents, no matter the abundance or lack of it in our homes, our job now is to be grateful for whatever it took to bring us to this moment in time because whatever the circumstance were, they were perfect for each of us.

To feel deprived, cheated, unfortunate, or ill-used as a result of our childhood circumstances is to declare ourselves unaware of the essential need for the very circumstances into which we were born and under which we were raised. It also forces us to carry a burden, to think of ourselves as victims, and it colors all the days of our lives a dull gray. It spoils the singing of the lark.

We must teach our children to see the opportunity for growth and change in their circumstances, no matter how rich or poor those circumstances may be, and we must teach them the necessity for having experienced those circumstances.

We all want to better our circumstances. It's like physically "working out." By bettering our circumstances, we gain strength, expand our awareness, and gain the benefit of living in a better environment.

If you feel yourself to be a victim of circumstances, free yourself of that burden now. Use the *I Ching* and the yarrow stalks to ask why you have experienced what you have. Discover the underlying need for whatever you experienced that is causing you pain.

It is very difficult for us to make the change from feeling victimized to feeling grateful for whatever has occurred in our lives, but we must do so if we are to see all occurrences in their proper light. Once we have accomplished that goal, we will then respond to new events in a way that sweeps away all obstacles before us, leaving our road clear and the sun shining. That major change in outlook will bring us the rewards of supreme good fortune and great success. That lesson is what we must teach our children.

For our children to become healthy-minded, strong adults, we must carefully nurture them. Hitting our children or screaming at them is absolutely to be avoided. Such acts not only deaden the child's sensitivity, they also teach the child to lose respect for the parent and destroy the possibility of any real closeness or communication between parent and child. The old maxim of "spare the rod and spoil the child" is barbaric.

Respect is not to be confused with fear. Hitting a child may induce fear, but respect can never be gained in that way.

In *I Ching Wisdom* it states:

> *Power*
> *best expresses itself*
> *in gentleness.*

wu wei's comment:

> The bully, the despot, and the person in authority who uses his power to hurt others are all universally disliked. They create their own unpleasant environment within which they must exist. By contrast, the superior person in a position of power can be clearly recognized by his gentleness. His gentle expression of power does not provoke resentment nor incur resistance, and so makes easy the attainment of his purposes and the continued growth of his power. By following the example of the superior person, you will go your way unopposed on a smooth, easy road.

For those of us who wield power and would like to have our power enrich us and those around us, we must be certain to only exercise our power in everyone's highest and best interest.

In *I Ching Wisdom* it states:

> *For power to be truly great*

*it must remain inwardly united
with the fundamental principles
of right and justice.*

wu wei's comment:

> The inferior person, concerned only for his own well being and pleasure, uses his power to further his own selfish ends and to cause hurt and trouble for others. This is degenerative use of power and bodes ill for everyone, particularly the wielder of the power. The superior person, concerned with the principles of right and justice, uses his power to aid others and improve the general welfare. This bodes well for everyone, particularly the wielder of the power.

When the power a parent has over a child is used incorrectly, the child develops in a warped manner. It is true that whatever the child experiences is in the child's best interests, but an aware parent, only uses power to act for the child, never against the child.

Because parents are stronger, quicker and better informed than their young children, they can always win over them. However, if we want our children to develop into winners, we must provide them with the experience of winning when they are children. In little foot races, in discussions, in will power struggles, and in many other ways, the child should be allowed to win. That course of action will have a tendency to make the child more difficult to handle, but if we want to raise children to be like fiery steeds rather than spiritless horses such as one uses to pull milk carts, we must allow them to win as children.

A child should be encouraged to reason with a parent. If we forbid a child to do something, and the child questions our decision or fights against it, we can powerfully overcome the child's protests, but failing to encourage the child to fight for what he wants may erode the child's will and program him to accept the dictates of others without question. He will also possibly fail to stand up for his rights later in life.

Children are told by their parents, "Do what I tell you to do," and later, "Do what the teacher tells you to do," and again, "Do what the baby sitter tells you to do." Fairly soon, the child does what everyone tells him to do, and we later wonder why our children did not grow into strong, independent people.

Neither should we pamper our children.

In *I Ching Wisdom* it states:

> *If one clings*
> *to the little boy,*
> *one loses*
> *the strong man.*

wu wei's comment:

At a point in your life you must leave behind your childish ideas and your need to cling to an adult if you are to become a strong, independent person. When you become a parent, if you pamper your

123

child, you will prevent the child from becoming a strong, independent person. You cannot help your children beyond a certain point without precluding their gaining strength on their own. Sometimes a loving parent is the most difficult hurdle a developing child has to overcome.

The desire to nurture can lead to indulgence. If we always carry our children, they will never develop their own muscles.

During the entire life of our children, we should use the *I Ching* for guidance about what to do in various circumstances. "What can I expect from enrolling my child in Forest Hills school?" "How will the new neighborhood affect my children?" "What can my daughter expect from a career as a doctor?" "How can my son solve his problem in school?" "How can I improve myself as a parent?" "How can I improve my relationship with my daughter?" "What counsel should I give my son regarding his current problem?" Using our divinitory

124

powers to seek guidance is one of the best ways to gain information about bringing up children.

In the hustle and bustle of earning a living and sorting out the day-to-day problems associated with our lives, we forget the reasons we are here on earth—to gain experience and to perfect ourselves as divine beings. We become caught up in the whirl of the senses and the press of the problems, forgetting our true missions—to perfect ourselves as divine beings and to impart that knowledge to our children.

How do we perfect ourselves? We keep aware of our missions. All else will occur as a result of natural law. The difference between living life aware of our missions and not aware is as dramatic as the difference between night and day. It is the difference between going through life with All-That-Is a knowing, cooperative, helping partner, and going through life alone, in a seemingly inert, dead, unresponsive Universe. I say "seemingly" because the Universe is not inert, dead or unresponsive, but if we are unaware of the life of the Universe, we will not consciously communicate with and interact with our Universe. Neither will we be aware off the subtle promptings of the Universe and may miss becoming aware of them, and we may not be aware that the events that are occurring in our lives are Universal occurrences that are for our benefit.

One of the most important messages we can give to our children is, "You can do it." Self-confidence gives our children the power to accomplish goals, to overcome fears, and to become who and what the children want. To that extent, we should encourage our children to take on ever greater tasks and ever greater responsibility, instilling in them the confidence that they can accomplish their goals. A constant message that we should give our children is "You can do it!"

Another way that we can build self confidence in our children is to trust them. Trust builds the child's self-respect and causes the child to respect us. We should also trust the child's judgment. By doing that, we will teach the child self-reliance. Children want us to trust them and have confidence in them. We build their morale when we extend our trust and our confidence to our children. It makes them feel important, loved, and dependable.

Last, we should not be overly critical of our children. They want us to see them as strong, capable, and reliable. If we hold that image of our children strongly in our minds, they will surely fulfill that image as a process of natural law. We are to hold that image no matter what befalls them, no matter if we are disappointed in them, no matter what they do, no matter what they say, and, as a result of that, our relationships with our children will be as strong as the gravity that holds the earth together and as lasting as Universal law.

CHAPTER THIRTEEN

WORK

Work is often thought of and spoken of as a distasteful chore, something we must do to earn money, to keep our homes clean, to take care of ourselves and others, to buy clothing and other essentials, and to provide ourselves with the wherewithal to have fun.

One of the most wonderful blessings that can befall any of us is to be able to earn a living doing what we love. Many of us work at jobs we do not care for. Either we are bound to a job we do not like by circumstances we believe to be insurmountable, or we believe we are unsuited by education, opportunity or talent to work in a field that would please us.

What is hard to believe is that we are not bound to work we dislike by circumstances, lack of opportunity, or lack of talent or education, but by our beliefs. We can change any of the circumstances of our lives, work included, but only if we believe we can change them. If we don't believe we can, we don't make the attempt.

A wonderful use of the *I Ching* and the yarrow stalks is to ask, "How can I get to do the work I love?" "What will happen if I leave my present employment and seek work elsewhere?" "What can I expect if I start my own business?" "What can I expect if I switch jobs?" "How can I earn more money?" "What can I do to improve myself so I can earn more money?" "How can I get ahead in my company?" What do I need to know about my job? "What can I expect if I seek work in another part of the state?" "What will happen if I ask for a raise?" "What will happen if I go over the head of my superior and complain about his poor work habits?" "What can I expect if I remain with my present employer?"

By far, most of the people I have met in my lifetime were working at some job or another that they did not particularly like, and, in some cases, actually hated. The reason they did not choose to do something else was specifically different for each person, but generally the same for everyone: fear; fear of loss of income, fear of not finding another job, fear of loss of seniority. The reasons were endless, but all of the reasons were based on fear. And, of course, they didn't believe they could make changes.

The fear that makes us hold onto one thing that sustains us before we have another to take its place stems from lack of confidence; lack of confidence in ourselves or lack of confidence in the Universe of which we are a part.

One of the major discoveries of my life is that if we trust the Universe, and act on the basis of that trust, we will not only achieve our goals, but for having acted out of trust, we will also receive the bonus benefit mentioned earlier

If you are in a work situation that is less than satisfying to you, resolve now to change it.

Remember that you are part of a glorious Universe that wants you to have the best of everything. If you fail to act on the basis of that belief, you are not living up to your potential as a great human being.

One of the most important concepts in working, is to do each task for its own sake, without regard to the reward we will receive for completing the task.

In *I Ching Wisdom* it states:

> Do not set your eyes on the harvest
> while planting it,
> nor on the use of the ground
> while clearing it.

wu wei's comment:

Every task must receive the attention it deserves if it is to turn out well. Anticipating the outcome of our efforts may cause us to become impatient and over-eager, hurrying to complete the task. Hasty or careless work will result in unsatisfactory performance of the task, which, of course, will bring about an unsatisfactory result. We should do every task for its own sake, do it as well as we can, and it can only happen that we will achieve good fortune and great success.

In the workplace, many of us desire to get ahead, to be in a position of leadership. By focusing our attention on doing each task that is assigned to us, and by fulfilling our duties conscientiously, we will achieve our goals as a consequence of natural law.

Before rising to positions of leadership, we are wise to ask ourselves what our motivation is. Most likely, our motivation is the additional income we will receive for taking on the additional responsibility, and, generally, a rise in position gives us more freedom and respect within the workplace. However, there are other reasons for rising to a position of leadership that will serve us well if we know of them and aspire to them.

In *I Ching Wisdom* it states:

> *If you would rule,*
> *first*
> *learn to serve.*

wu wei's comment:

By first learning to serve, you will come to understand those who will eventually serve you. The only valid reason for a superior person to want to rule is so he can better serve those whom he rules. If you are unprepared or unwilling to serve your followers, it is better for them, and for you, that you never achieve rulership because if you do and then cease to serve them, you will lose your following. All your efforts will have been for naught, and you will suffer great embarrassment. Only through serving can you obtain from those whom you rule the joyous assent that is necessary if they are to follow you.

Use the *I Ching* to ask, "What can I expect from taking on a position of leadership?" "What do I need to know about leading my fellow workers?"

Once you are in a position of power, find a use for everyone and everything. In this way you will be loved and respected, and your power will blossom, carrying you to ever greater heights.

In *I Ching Wisdom* it states:

> *In the hands of a great master,*
> *all material is productive.*

wu wei's comment:

> He can find a use for everything and everyone. He wastes nothing; therefore, he always has enough. He values everyone; therefore, everyone values him.

Whatever our work is, we should do it as if we were doing it for ourselves, for our own benefit. We should not complain that the work is tedious or that we are doing more than another and being paid less or that our employer doesn't care for the employees. We are children of the Universe. If we are generous with ourselves and our time, the Universal law of cause and effect will amply reward us. If we begrudge ourselves or our time, the Universal law of cause and effect will take its toll. Giving generously of ourselves and our time, relying on the Universe to reward us, will cause us to move through our work as though drawn by six strong horses.

CHAPTER FOURTEEN

GAIN AND LOSS

In *I Ching Wisdom* it states:

> *Take not gain or loss to heart.*
> *What man holds high*
> *comes to nothing.*

wu wei's comment:

> You are not your gain; neither are you
> your loss. Gain and loss are external to
> you, things with which your eternal soul is
> not concerned. All gains and losses pass
> away at the time of death. Do not waste
> even a moment on gains and losses
> when death is plucking your ears saying,
> "Live! I am coming."

The above saying and comment is the essence
of what there is to say about gains and losses.
The way we view gains, losses, and the
unfolding of events is critical to our success
and our happiness. To gain and hold that view,

consider the next saying.

In *I Ching Wisdom* it states:

> *A situation only becomes favorable
> when one adapts to it.*

wu wei's comment:

As long as we are angry or upset over an event, we will be unable to perceive its beneficial aspects, and we may wear ourselves out with unnecessary resistance; the event may have been to our complete advantage from the first moment. Even happy turns of fortune sometimes come to us in a form that seems strange or unlucky. The event itself is simply an event; the way we respond to the event determines its final outcome in our lives. Once an event has taken place, since we cannot alter the past, all that is left to us is our responses. Why not respond as though the event occurred for our benefit? We will then immediately experience good feelings about the event, and by acting in accord with our feelings, we will help to bring about that end. All of us who understand that concept and act accordingly will mount through the skies of success as though on the wings of six dragons.

If you sustain a loss or experience some hurtful occurrence, it is well to keep in mind what is still left to you.

In *I Ching Wisdom* it states:

> *Do not complain.*
> *Enjoy the good fortune*
> *you still possess.*

wu wei's comment:

In an undesirable situation or confronted with a loss, the inferior person bitterly complains and curses his luck. The superior person remembers the good things still left to him and smiles. He knows that the seemingly undesirable situation or loss will ultimately be a benefit to him; thus, he responds in a positive way. One is sad; one is glad. Each is in charge of his response; each has set the pattern for the continuing course of events.

We are in charge of the way we feel about things. Too many times we do not control our reactions to events. We react on the spur of the moment, without thinking; we react out of hurt or fear or surprise; we react out of indignation or pride. Remember that we are part of the Universe. Remember that the Universe is well inclined, beneficially inclined. Remember that everything that happens will ultimately benefit us. Remembering those things will cause us to react to the ever unfolding events of the Universe in a positive manner which, in itself, is already a benefit and will bring us good fortune and great success.

Oftentimes we are led into doing something that is not in keeping with the actions of a superior person to obtain something we want. Before we take those kinds of actions, we should each ask: "What can I expect from taking that action?"

In *I Ching Wisdom* it states:

> *If*
> *you are not dazzled by enticing goals,*
> *and*
> *remain true to yourself,*
> *you will travel through life*
> *unassailed,*
> *on a level road.*

wu wei's comment:

Great riches or enticements that dazzle us may also cause us to attempt to get them by means that are inappropriate to the superior person. Such actions always lead to remorse. If we remain true to ourselves, if we live up to the best within ourselves, we will walk the path of the superior person and, in so doing, will reap the rewards of a prince and the glory of a king.

The rewards of a prince and the glory of a king are truly wonderful gifts, not to be thought

142

lightly of as a phrase this writer has tossed off. Everything you read here is deliberately written and is meant to be taken literally. The rewards of a prince and the glory of a king are not necessarily material things—although they may be. There are things much more to be sought after than material things which, in time, become nothing.

In *I Ching Wisdom* it states:

> *Even the finest clothes*
> *turn to rags.*

wu wei's comment:

Everything, the moment it is made, begins to decay. Is it wise, therefore, to set much store in finery and other such objects? The superior person does not attach great importance to things that decay. He does attach great importance to those things which endure: his integrity, his honor, his virtue, and his appreciation and reverence for All-That-Is. That is not to say that we should not value our possessions, for they bring us much pleasure, but that we should not set great store by them, for they are transitory, and there are other, greater treasures.

We have already received the greatest gift of all: we are part of this glorious Universe. In the face of that, everything else is inconsequential. Looked at in the context of "right here and right now," we can see ourselves as sustaining losses, being hurt, rejected, ill used, or unlucky. Looked at over the course of eternity, which is what constitutes our outer limits, all of this lifetime is less than one trillionth of the beat of a humming bird's wing, and those things that cause us distress are truly inconsequential. In actuality, they are for our benefit. Our job is to see them in that light and deal with them in that way. Use the I Ching to inquire, "Why am I experiencing this unpleasant situation?"

On our way to perfecting ourselves as divine beings, all the material gains and losses we experience are of no more consequence than the flutter of an eyelash. The way in which we deal with them is of great consequence for it is the mark of our spiritual progress or lack of it.

CHAPTER FIFTEEN

RECOVERY

What is recovery if not the return to health after sickness, the return to strength after weakness, a regaining of balance after imbalance, a return to wholeness after impairment, the return of a possession after a loss, the return of hope after a time of despair, the return of love after a time of its absence, the return of joy after sorrow?

Kua 24, Fu, Return, is made up of five broken lines over one unbroken line (☷). All the lines of a *kua* enter the *kua* from the bottom, move through the six stages of change, and leave again at the top. The broken lines represent the dark force, the unbroken lines represent the light force. *Kua* 24, Fu, Return, shows a light force line entering from the bottom. Prior to the new line entering from the bottom, all the lines were dark force lines, representing a time of darkness. Now, we have

"Return," an unbroken line entering from the bottom, and it signifies a return of the light force. This *kua* could also be called "Recovery," because of its meaning.

The *kua*, Fu, tells us that after all periods of darkness comes a time of light, that after all despair comes hope, that after a loss comes gain. There is always renewal.

In *I Ching Wisdom* it states:

> *No plain not followed by a slope,*
> *no increase not followed by a decrease.*

wu wei's comment:

It is an eternal law of the universe that everything, when it reaches its maximum potential, turns toward its opposite. Knowing this law, the superior person provides for a time of decrease in times of prosperity. He builds himself up during times of good health and so prepares against a time of illness. He takes precautions in times of safety that protect him in times of danger. He thinks ahead and, in so doing, is prepared. He thereby enjoys a lifetime of good fortune and success.

All of us who lose a loved one are but a half-step in time away from following the loved one. As stated elsewhere in this book, there are only two possibilities open to us when our time here on earth is over: we either retain our individuality and continue evolving, or we are reabsorbed into the totality of the Universe. Either end is magnificent.

During our remaining time here on earth, we should keep a bright outlook. Be cheerful. The Universe would not crown this wonderful life with a bad ending. Use the *I Ching* and ask, "What can I expect after I pass on from this life?"

In *I Ching Wisdom* it states:

> *Waiting*
> *should not be*
> *mere empty hoping;*

it should be filled with
the inner certainty
of reaching the goal.

wu wei's comment:

Uncertain of reaching our goal, our
waiting will be filled with worrying and
fearful imaginings, both of which are
detrimental to productivity and lead away
from success. Certain of reaching our
goal, our waiting will be filled with happy
thoughts and useful occupation, both of
which lead directly to success.

In *I Ching Wisdom* it states:

Every ending contains a new beginning.

wu wei's comment:

Even the longest journey only started by
the first step. No matter how poor our
circumstances are, no matter how poor
our personal conditions are, the path of
the superior person, which only leads to
supreme good fortune and great success,
is always directly in front of us. We may

take the first step upon it at any time and magically transform our circumstances. These benefits are available to everyone, withheld from no one. The path of the inferior person is also always directly in front of us, bringing its lessons of hardship, misery and despair, but only so that we will ultimately come to know the truth. At each step of our way we must always choose between those two paths. The ending of one path always means the beginning of the other. We must choose well; our future is entirely in our own hands.

The Universe is an ever changing, ever nurturing Being. Remember the first half of Chapter One:

"The same intelligent, aware force that created and sustains the Universe, that *is* the Universe, created and sustains us. That intelligent, creative, aware force endlessly shapes and alters us, changes us, to the purpose that we will ultimately come to achieve our true nature and thereafter will keep us forever resonating with the great harmony."

Our gains and losses are part of the beneficial fluctuation of the Universe. It is well for us to remember that all decrease is followed by increase, all loss by gain, and all sorrow by joy. That is the way.

CHAPTER SIXTEEN

HEALTH

Whenever we meet someone who has obvious good health, he or she almost always has a cheerful countenance and a good outlook on life. If we were to ask the next hundred people we meet what the most important thing in life is, good health would always be near the top, if not at the top, of everyone's list.

Good health mainly comes from what we hold in our mind as thoughts. A healthy body is the product of a healthy mind.

In *I Ching Wisdom* it states:

> *Those things in our psychic body*
> *later manifest*
> *in our physical body.*

wu wei's comment:

The mind is a creator, and what we hold there manifests itself in one way or another. If we hold worrying and stress in our minds, they will manifest themselves in our bodies as tension and pain. If we hold thankfulness and joy in our minds, they will manifest themselves in our bodies as radiant health and shining countenances.

Our habits play a crucial role in maintaining abundant good health. Once we cultivate a good habit, it is almost effortless to maintain it. Cleanliness, for instance, plays a major role in keeping healthy. If we train ourselves to be personally clean and to keep the environment clean in which we live and work, it becomes almost effortless to maintain a state of cleanliness.

We are heavily influenced by our surroundings. If we keep our environment neat and orderly, it will cause a healthy condition to exist in our minds and, therefore, in our bodies. It's like a reflection. In actuality, the way we keep ourselves and our surroundings is a direct result, a reflection, of what goes on inside our minds.

Imagine for a moment that you are living in a home that is not clean and is not neat. Now imagine that, having read this, you clean your home and make it neat. In that case, it is easy to see that your mind has had an effect on your surroundings.

What is not so easy to see, but which works the same way in reverse, is that when you live in a clean, neat home, it affects your mind. Your surroundings affect your mind the way your mind affects your surroundings. Knowing that, you can reap the great rewards that accompany cleanliness and neatness by making it a habit to be so.

In *I Ching Wisdom* it states:

> *In cultivating oneself,*
> *it is best to root out bad habits*
> *and tolerate those that are harmless.*

wu wei's comment:

> If we are too weak to overcome habits
> that are obviously bad for us, our futures
> are indeed bleak. While temporary
> pleasures may accompany bad habits,
> they are, in the long run, detrimental to us
> and even in the short run weaken us.
> Acquiring a long-run problem in exchange
> for a short-run pleasure is not a good
> bargain. It takes strength and
> determination to rid ourselves of bad
> habits that control us, but by so doing, we
> gain control, increase our strength, and
> have better lives. A superior person is
> always in control of his habits. To be
> successful in rooting out bad habits, it is,
> however, wise to tolerate harmless habits
> for a time; if we are too strict with
> ourselves, we may fail in our purposes.

All acts are a product of our intentions, and,
therefore, if we have taken the time to cultivate
good intentions, our acts will reflect those good
intentions. Good intentions, like good habits,

are of tremendous benefit to us.

In *I Ching Wisdom* it states:

> *To be a superior person,*
> *see to it*
> *that goodness*
> *is an established attribute of character*
> *rather than*
> *an accidental and isolated occurrence.*

wu wei's comment:

True goodness means that our intentions are always beneficial, never hurtful. To maintain our beneficial intentions, it is necessary to renew our determination every day to follow the path of the superior person, always working to improve our characters. For persevering in our efforts, we will find within ourselves a wellspring of joy that will refresh and renew us all of our days, and good fortune and success will surely come.

To have good health, it is essential that we alternate periods of activity with periods of rest.

In *I Ching Wisdom* it states:

> *If you live in a state of perpetual hurry,*
> *you will fail to attain inner composure.*

wu wei's comment:

Inner composure means having a settled state of mind; calmness, tranquillity. Whoever attains this state is then able to act without stress and therefore makes no mistakes. Constant hurrying wears us down, destroys calmness, and puts lines in our faces. By slowing ourselves and nurturing ourselves with the ways of the superior person, all else will be achieved through the process of natural law.

We can achieve good health using the *I Ching* as a guide. We can ask questions such as: "What can I do to achieve optimal health?" "How can I overcome my current illness?" "What should I be paying attention to now with regard to my health?" "What can I expect if I become a vegetarian?" "How will a move to a drier climate effect my health?" "How is my current relationship affecting my health?" What will happen if I continue my habit of smoking cigarettes?" "How can I overcome my habit of eating too much?"

All the answers are at our disposal. By asking sincerely and with reverence, everything will be revealed to us.

CHAPTER SEVENTEEN

BUSINESS

To engage in business is to work for a profit. This chapter will deal with those who are "in business," meaning those who have undertaken an endeavor in the hope of earning a profit. That is not to say that a wage earner cannot benefit by the wisdom. Quite the contrary. He can use the wisdom to dramatically enhance his own chances for success and, also, if he properly applies the wisdom, can use it to successfully start in business for himself.

Whenever we are in business, we deal with people, and so a successful business necessarily deals successfully with people.

Of course, the most important aspect of being in business has to do with our characters. If our characters are flawed, either our enterprises are doomed to failure or the profits from the business will in some way work against us.

Neither will we be able to enjoy our business, but will encounter endless problems. The problems will seem to be caused by outside influences, but that is not the case. We constantly affect everything and everyone around us by being the way we are at every moment.

In *I Ching Wisdom* it states:

> *The superior person*
> *spends a lifetime*
> *developing strong character,*
> *and so*
> *enjoys a lifetime*
> *of supreme good fortune*
> *and great success.*

wu wei's comment:

A tree on a mountain develops slowly, according to the law of its being, and consequently stands firmly rooted. So also, the development of one's character must undergo gradual development if it is to have a broad, stable base. The very

163

gradualness of the development makes it necessary, however, to have perseverance lest slow progress become stagnation. For being successful in our efforts, we, also, will enjoy a lifetime of supreme good fortune and great success.

There are many ways that we can use the *I Ching* in business. For instance, before we undertake a business venture we can ask, "What aspect of my character needs developing so I can be successful in business?" "What can I expect from this new business venture?' "What will happen if I take a partner?" "What can I expect from this merger?" "What can I expect from taking on this new product line?" "What do I have to be careful of in this new venture?" "Will I be successful in this business?" "What will be the result if I apply for a business loan?" "What can I expect if I move my business to another location?" "What can I expect if I expand my business?"

In all ventures, there is one constant: ourselves.

People come and go; events transpire and pass away; everything concerning our venture changes, but we remain. Therefore, we must be able to depend on ourselves if we are to succeed. Even though we may be just starting in business with little or no expertise and little or no capital, we can succeed by following the wisdom in the *I Ching*.

In *I Ching Wisdom* it states:

> *You can succeed in life,*
> *no matter your circumstances,*
> *provided*
> *you have determination*
> *and follow*
> *the path of the superior person.*

wu wei's comment:

The opportunities to achieve success are endless, and even those who start with nothing can succeed, but even the finest opportunity in the wrong hands comes to nothing. All that is necessary to achieve success, great success, is to cultivate perseverance as an established trait of character and to follow the path of the superior person. By accomplishing that we will speed to our success as eagles in flight.

Of course, it helps to be smart, too, but even people who aren't smart can succeed. It does not take intelligence to get answers from the Universe; it takes sincerity and reverence. Anyone who is sincere and approaches his questioning with sincerity and reverence will get correct answers that are entirely in his best interest.

Because the world and all that is in it is constantly changing, to be successful, we too, must change.

In *I Ching Wisdom* it states:

> *To be successful,*
> *do not be rigid and immobile*
> *in your thinking,*
> *but always keep abreast of the time*
> *and*

change with it.

wu wei's comment:

> The universal law that provides for constant change is the only thing that does not change. To remain inflexible when all else is changing is to invite disaster. It is essential to our success that we set firm courses and that we be stable enough in our characters not to waver with every passing fad; it is equally essential, however, that we be aware of changing conditions and be open and flexible enough in our thinking to change with changing conditions. Maintaining rigidity leads to failure; remaining flexible leads to success.

As we near the pinnacle of success, we must stay alert. We must remember the Universal law that states that everything, when it reaches its maximum potential, turns toward its opposite.

In *I Ching Wisdom* it states:

*On the road to success,
as you near the attainment of your goal,
beware of becoming intoxicated
with your achievement.*

wu wei's comment:

If we allow ourselves to become overly
excited about an approaching success,
we may become careless or light-headed
and fail to pay attention to crucial matters
and thereby ruin our success. It is
precisely at the point of success that we
must remain sober and cautious. By
maintaining the attitude and course of
action that brought us to the point of
success, we will surely and safely arrive
at our goals.

Modesty and conscientiousness also play a
major role in business, particularly when we
are just starting.

In *I Ching Wisdom* it states:

*Exceptional
modesty and conscientiousness*

are sure to be rewarded

with

great success

and

good fortune

wu wei's comment:

Being modest means that we have cultivated humble attitudes and we do not give ourselves airs or strut around trying to impress people; nor are we boastful of our accomplishments. Being conscientious means that we fulfill our tasks and obligations with great care. If we are exceptionally modest and conscientious in a high position, our radiance will be like the sun at mid-day, and no blame will attach to our progress. The attainment of our goals will be rapid and easy. If we are exceptionally modest and conscientious and hold a low position, we will be recognized and rewarded, and we will rise quickly through the ranks.

When we first start in business, it is essential that we have a plan. As we progress, it may be necessary to modify the plan in the face of unforeseen circumstances, but to begin without a clear plan is to invite disaster.

In *I Ching Wisdom* it states:

Exceptional enterprises cannot succeed unless the utmost caution is observed in their beginnings.

wu wei's comment:

In the beginning of even small things, exceptional care must be exercised if a planting is to lead to a flowering. How much more then should exceptional care be exercised when great or dangerous undertakings are begun? A flaw, built into the beginning, increases with time, and if not corrected, will ultimately cause the failure of the enterprise. The superior person can always see the end in the beginning; he knows the seeds and, exercising great care, enjoys a lifetime of

170

success and good fortune.

While you are in business, you will be called upon to make many decisions. Using the *I Ching* to inquire about a correct course of action is of inestimable benefit. Once you have made your inquiry, carefully consider your options and then act. Opportunities have often been lost through inaction.

In *I Ching Wisdom* it states:

> *After a matter*
> *has been thoroughly considered,*
> *it is essential*
> *to form a decision*
> *and*
> *to act.*

wu wei's comment:

Reflection or pondering must not be carried too far, lest either cripple the power of decision. When the time for action has come, the moment must be seized. Once a matter has been thoroughly considered, anxious hesitation is a mistake that is bound to bring disaster because you will have missed your opportunity.

Being in business almost necessarily means we will encounter conflict—conflict with employees, business competitors, and others with whom we transact business. In times of such conflict, it is always better to settle the argument quickly and proceed to more productive affairs than to continue the conflict.

In *I Ching Wisdom* it states:

> *When entangled in a conflict*
> *it is wise*
> *to remain so clear headed and strong*
> *that you are always ready*
> *to come to terms with your opponent*
> *by meeting him halfway.*

wu wei's comment:

In times of conflict we are always in danger because our opponents are seeking to harm us. Taking an opportunity to end the conflict by meeting our opponents half-way leads away from a time of conflict to a time of security. That is a wise and sensible course of action, and the superior person seizes the opportunity, knowing that, in truth, he has won a great victory. To carry on a conflict to the bitter end has evil effects because the enmity is then continued.

If we find ourselves embroiled in a conflict with a far stronger adversary, we should not use up all our resources fighting a battle that we have only a poor chance of winning. If we are unable to negotiate a settlement, we should withdraw.

In *I Ching Wisdom* it states:

When confronted with insurmountable forces retreat is proper.

wu wei's comment:

If we persist in fighting a battle that is beyond our capabilities, we risk depleting our resources so greatly that we cannot recover. To retreat does not mean to give up the battle. On the contrary, retreating preserves our resources and allows us time to regain our strength, renew our forces, and make new plans. Thus, retreat makes possible a counter-movement, which makes possible our success.

During our entire business life, we should use our higher powers to consult with All-That-Is to find our best courses of action. Even when our business is flourishing, we should ask, "Is there anything I should be paying attention to now?" There may be an unforeseen danger that is approaching. Using the *I Ching*, we can alert ourselves to the danger and either prepare for it or avert it completely.

CHAPTER EIGHTEEN

WEALTH

Once we have achieved wealth, we then want to protect it. Because of the Universal law of increase and decrease, one following the other, the *I Ching* advises that it is wise to distribute our wealth while we are accumulating it. Doing that will lengthen our times of increase.

There is other wisdom in the *I Ching* that can assist us in preserving and increasing our wealth. For instance, we will encounter ineptitude, carelessness, or deliberate transgressions on the part of people who are in our employ or with whom we are associated or with whom we are transacting business. If we take these people to task for their actions, we risk disturbing the successful flow of our business affairs.

In *I Ching Wisdom* it states:

In times of prosperity
it is important
to possess enough greatness of spirit
to bear with the mistakes of others.

wu wei's comment:

Just as water washes everything clean,
the superior person pardons mistakes
and even forgives intentional
transgressions. In that way he insures
the upward spiral of his prosperity. The
inferior person cannot resist the
opportunity to chastise another and, in so
doing, incurs resentment, destroys
unanimity, and crushes enthusiasm,
thereby destroying his own chances for
success.

Of course, there are times when it is necessary
to reprimand someone or even terminate our
association with someone, but we should give
careful thought to such actions before taking
them.

To preserve wealth, it is essential that we be

thrifty. The wisdom of the *I Ching* cautions us that the superior person does not overreach himself, overspend himself, or strive foolishly.

In *I Ching Wisdom* it states:

> In financial matters,
> well being prevails
> when expenditures and income
> are in proportion.

wu wei's comment:

Out of debt; out of danger. We should not spend more than we have; credit enslaves. Since all periods of prosperity are followed by periods of decline, the superior person prepares for the times of decline during the times of prosperity. If we always spend all that we have, we will be unprepared in times of emergency. Such poor planning leads to the destruction of well-being and invites disaster.

In keeping with that, it is prudent to cut back on expenditures. Cutting back on expenditures may cause us to appear miserly, selfish, or poor, and while that feeling might make us uncomfortable, it may be necessary to preserve what we have.

In *I Ching Wisdom* it states:

> *Do not be ashamed*
> *of*
> *simplicity*
> *or*
> *small means.*

wu wei's comment:

Simplicity is the hallmark of the superior person, ostentation, the hallmark of the inferior person. If we are following the path of the superior person we are the equal of any person on earth. There is no need, therefore, to present false appearances; even with slender means, or no means at all, the sentiments of our hearts can be expressed. It is not for the value of our gifts that we are appreciated, but for the sentiments with which they are

given and the value we hold in the eyes of
the receivers.

Being wealthy carries with it the obligation that
we do not use our wealth to make others feel
inadequate or less fortunate than ourselves.
Making a show of wealth is one of the surest
ways to lose it. Remember that we live in and
are part of an aware Universe. To hurt one part
of the Universe, someone else, with another
part, ourselves, will surely cause a problem for
the part that is doing the hurting. If, in the case
of making a display of our wealth, we are the
ones making the display, we can be sure that
some form of correction will follow. Not
correction to hurt or punish, but to teach; the
Universe will never act against its own best
interests.

Having wealth often encourages people who
are in need to approach us for help. If we
indiscriminately give to all who ask, we will
shortly be without wealth ourselves.
Therefore, it is wise to take each case

separately, and to look deeply into each situation before we decide on a course of action. Rarely is it a good course of action to give money to someone who has not earned it. If one has not earned the money, it will more than likely hurt that person rather than help them. However, there is a bit of wisdom in the *I Ching* that pertains to that aspect of wealth.

In *I Ching Wisdom* it states:

> *Through hardness and selfishness,*
> *the heart grows rigid,*
> *and this rigidity*
> *leads to*
> *separation from others.*

wu wei's comment:

When we see someone in need and turn away from him, that is the beginning of hardness. When someone asks us for help, and we refuse, selfishly hoarding what we have, the hardness grows. When someone asks us for forgiveness, and we refuse, that is the beginning of rigidity. Soon, we begin to look at everyone from behind masks of hardness. That is our protection against their plea for help. Our voices become sharp, and our manner truculent. Everyone avoids us except the hangers-on who are after the few crumbs that fall from our tables. Hardness and selfishness are characteristics of the inferior person. Gentleness and generosity are characteristics of the superior person. Hardness and selfishness, gentleness and generosity; they each bring their own inevitable results.

It takes great wisdom to handle wealth correctly. Having achieved it, we are subject to the law that will remove the wealth from us if we misuse it. Furthermore, we must have wisdom to overcome the fear of losing whatever wealth we have gained.

In *I Ching Wisdom* it states:

> *It is only after*
> *perfect balance*

has been achieved
that any misstep
brings imbalance.

wu wei's comment:

It is only after the achievement of success, wealth, fame, happiness, love, popularity, or possessions that we can be burdened with the fear of losing them. This is a caution that we are to remain modest and vigilant once we have acquired our treasure, whatever it is, or the same law that brought it to us will remove it from us or cause it to work to our detriment. We should not delude ourselves that our achievements and possessions are the end-all be-all of life. They are merely the objects we have chosen to lead ourselves along the path of life. It is the path itself that is the end-all be-all, for on that path we shall learn the lessons of life and perfect ourselves as divine incarnations.

If we would protect our wealth once we have

accumulated it, we must be as cautious as a fox crossing thin ice in our display of wealth and in the ways we use it.

Setting up a trust to provide income for our children is a great error. It deprives them of the incentive to work, without which, no one can be happy. I have never seen it work to the advantage of a child to be left a large sum of money, unless the child has participated for many years in the earning of that money and has learned how to use it before receiving it.

One of the most important aspects of wealth is knowing when we have enough. A sane person will set limits on the amount of wealth he accumulates. Once we have achieved enough wealth so that we can follow other pursuits, we should stop putting forth the effort to accumulate wealth.

What generally happens is that we keep escalating our standard of living and the gratification of our desires to match or run slightly ahead of our income. This is madness and will keep us on the treadmill for the rest of our lives. Some of us justify the continuation of the accumulation of wealth by saying, "I like what I do for a living." That may well be, but there are other more important matters for us to turn our attention to once we have accomplished our goal of financial security. What we can do without is oftentimes more important than the fulfillment of our desires.

We should set certain bounds for ourselves, within which we can experience complete freedom. It is a wise person who knows when he has enough.

In *I Ching Wisdom* it states:

> *Unlimited possibilities*
> *are not suited to mankind.*
> *If they existed,*
> *his life would only dissolve*
> *into the boundless.*

wu wei's comment:

Who is it that could choose among unlimited possibilities? Just to consider them would take all of eternity. Limitations are troublesome, but they are effective. The superior person sets limits within which he experiences total freedom. In so doing, he achieves focus and success and avoids danger.

Read those words carefully for in them is a message more precious than the wealth we seek.

We should use the *I Ching* to seek guidance in matters of wealth. "What can I expect if I stop accumulating wealth?" "To what should I turn my attention at this time?" "What will result if I give money to Harry/Susan?" What action should I take with regard to Harry's/Susan's request for money?" "What will result for my children if I leave them my wealth?"

CHAPTER NINETEEN

STILLNESS

In the midst of all activity, there must be a quiet time, a time for contemplation, a time for input.

In *I Ching Wisdom* it states:

> *In order to achieve a quiet heart,*
> *rest and movement*
> *must follow each other*
> *in accordance*
> *with the demands of the time.*

wu wei's comment:

Achieving a quiet heart allows us to be sensitive to the subtle promptings from the world around us, which, in turn, allows us to move effortlessly and smoothly through life rather than with great effort and blundering. Acting in accord with the demands of the time produces harmony. If, however, we are still when the time for action comes, we will miss our opportunity, and what would have been easy to achieve becomes difficult. Or if we are in motion during the time for rest, we will be unprepared when the time for action comes . The superior person first achieves a quiet heart, and then acts. Whoever acts from these deep levels makes no mistakes.

It is true that we can and do receive information from the Universe in a continuous stream. However, we can increase and improve our communication by deliberately making time available when we can be quiet without being interrupted. At the beginning of each of those times, we should avoid thinking of the things that trouble us: worries, business, money problems, and the like. Instead, we should remain relaxed and receptive. During those times it is good to think about the wisdom of the *I Ching*. Carrying this book and reading one of the sayings is a good way to begin. After that, lightly hold the thoughts in your mind about what you have read, and soon the flow will begin.

Once we have started the proper flow of communication, the answers we need for our most pressing questions will come to us. We must remember where the answers are coming from; remember that we are part of that; remember that the Universe is well inclined, beneficially inclined, that it wants to benefit itself—in this case, us—and just relax. The answers to our most difficult questions will come to us; we must trust those answers.

In *I Ching Wisdom* it states:

> *Once you have gained*
> *inner mastery of a problem,*
> *it will come about naturally*
> *that the action you take*
> *will succeed.*

wu wei's comment:

Gaining inner mastery of a problem begins with our recognition that the problem presents an opportunity for improving ourselves. Thinking our ways through the problem, keeping in mind that the solution will put us in better circumstances than before or prevent us from making an error will result in the success of any action we take.

If we set aside a time for meditation and find it difficult to quiet our thoughts, we should not force ourselves in any way, but should simply remain calm and gently push the thoughts away, turning our thoughts to one of the bits of wisdom in the *I Ching*.

In *I Ching Wisdom* it states:

> *In exercises in meditation*
> *and concentration,*
> *trying to force results*
> *will lead to an unwholesome outcome.*

wu wei's comment:

Trying to obtain by force that which can only be obtained by relaxation and calmness will produce results opposite from the ones you hope to achieve. By first achieving inner composure, you can develop meditation and concentration naturally, thereby producing the desired result.

To achieve stillness, we should cultivate moderation in our habits. Overeating, drinking too much alcohol, incessant talking, and general agitation are all detrimental to achieving stillness.

In *I Ching Wisdom* it states:

> *Words are movements*
> *going from within, outward.*
> *Eating and drinking are movements*
> *that go from without, inward.*
> *Both movements can be modified by*
> *tranquillity.*

wu wei's comment:

Tranquillity means being calm and peaceful. Everything, in its proper measure, benefits us. The same thing, carried to excess, destroys us. The way to achieve tranquillity is to follow the path of the superior person who is careful of his words and temperate in eating and drinking.

To achieve true detachment, we must remain calm. Passionate outbursts and uncontrolled fury never lead to stillness. Such occasions cause great turmoil in our minds which may take many hours and sometimes days to subside.

In *I Ching Wisdom* it states:

> *Passion and reason*
> *cannot exist side by side.*

wu wei's comment:

When anger, lust, hatred, or love consumes us, clear, rational thinking is impossible. It is only when we are able calmly to step back from ourselves and "look in on ourselves" that true detachment is achieved, which then permits rational thinking.

Stillness is a great treasure. Being still allows

us to perceive the greatness of the Universe. It is through stillness that we can feel our oneness with All-That-Is. Be still.

CHAPTER TWENTY

PERSONAL GOALS

We do not have to be powerful to achieve our goals. Neither must we have a strong position in life to succeed. What is necessary is that we know the Universal laws of achieving goals.

In *I Ching Wisdom* it states:

> *Even*
> *small power,*
> *used correctly,*
> *can achieve great success.*

wu wei's comment:

To use small power correctly: first, fix the goal firmly in your mind; see it clearly; imagine yourself attaining it; second, commit yourself to reaching the goal; third, use whatever power you have to always move in the direction of attainment, taking every opportunity that comes along and turning it to your advantage. Your perseverance must never slacken. Just as dripping water wears away the hardest rock, you will eventually arrive at your goal. To accomplish a great goal with a only a small amount of power is a wonderful accomplishment and brings you great respect, good fortune, and supreme success. Your power will then blossom, and you will accomplish other, greater deeds.

It does not matter who or what we are, we can succeed. There are a few bits of knowledge and wisdom that are of great help in attaining personal goals. One of the most important is to be modest.

In *I Ching Wisdom* it states:

> *By manifesting a humble attitude,*
> *people will naturally want to help you*
> *and give you good counsel.*

wu wei's comment:

It is a part of human nature to love and

help the humble and to resent and thwart the arrogant. People soon give up counseling an egotistical person who thinks he knows everything.

On the road to obtaining personal goals, being modest will benefit us immensely. Every time we depart from modesty, the law of cause and effect will bring us down. It's gratifying to boast of our achievements, but it always works against us.

In *I Ching Wisdom* it states:

> *Boasting of*
> *power, wealth, position, promotion, success, or*
> *influential friends*
> *inevitably*
> *invites misfortune and humiliation.*

wu wei's comment:

Boasting only confirms that we feel inferior, inadequate, and insecure and that we are trying to add to our statures by our boasting. The superior person considers what he has sufficient and lets it speak for itself. He acts modestly and in that way assures his continued success.

Before undertaking any serious goal, we should not make any boasts or claims because they bring resistance from those who hear us. It is the way of Universal law to bring down the high and uplift the lowly. We can see that law at work in the way mountains are worn down and valleys are filled up.

In *I Ching Wisdom* it states:

> *At the beginning of a project,*
> *if many boastful claims are made,*
> *the successful attainment of the goal*
> *becomes*
> *far more difficult.*

wu wei's comment:

When no claims are put forward, no resistance arises. If we cultivate modesty, we will make swift, sure progress because no resentment will attach to us. If we remain modest despite our merit, we will be beloved and will win the support necessary to carry out even difficult and dangerous undertakings. When we make boastful claims, even if we are moderately successful but fall short of our claims, people will say that we failed.

To achieve goals, we must take every opportunity that comes our way and use each opportunity to move closer to the attainment of our goal.

In *I Ching Wisdom* it states:

Not a whole day.

wu wei's comment:

An admonition from the *I Ching*. It means that when the superior person perceives that action is required, he does not let even a whole day pass before taking the required action.

Achieving goals brings us satisfaction in addition to the reward of the goal. There may be praise, for instance, if anyone knows of our achievement, or there may be an increase in our own strength. However, even the greatest goal will come to nothing if we are walking the path of the inferior person.

In *I Ching Wisdom* it states:

> If
> you are not as you should be
> you will have misfortune,
> and
> it does not further you
> to undertake
> anything.

wu wei's comment:

The path of the inferior person is filled with pitfalls of his own making. In any plan or undertaking of which we conceive, there is always one constant: ourselves. If our characters are flawed, if we cannot depend upon ourselves to be efficient or careful or cautious or persevering, then we are a danger and a detriment to our own plans, and it does not profit us to undertake anything. If our characters are without flaw, we can carry out even difficult and dangerous undertakings without fear of failure.

Sometimes, when we see a goal in front of us, we are tempted to take it by force, particularly if that is within our capability. Obtaining anything by force never benefits us in the end.

In *I Ching Wisdom* it states:

> *It is wise and reasonable*
> *not to try to obtain anything*
> *by force.*

wu wei's comment:

That which is obtained by force must be held by force. That constant exertion drains our powers, invites the censure of others, and inevitably leads to regret. It is a law of the universe that what we obtain by force will ultimately bring us misfortune in one form or another, and a superior person will have none of it. It may appear that something obtained by force is a temporary benefit to the person who obtained it, but in the end, the law will be fulfilled.

On the way to the achievement of our goals, we must be cautious and avoid conflict with those with whom we are have joined forces to achieve a goal. Even under the best of circumstances, it is difficult to achieve great goals. How much more difficult would it be to achieve a goal if we were fighting with our associates?

We should not be undecided about our actions when the time for action is at hand. The achievement of our goals requires our complete effort, the complete force of our intention without hesitation. If we are undecided or unsure of our actions, we will be unable to act with our full power.

In *I Ching Wisdom* it states:

> *Conflict within*
> *weakens the power to conquer*

danger without.

wu wei's comment:

> When the time for action has come, conflict within an individual will cause him to hesitate. Conflict within a group will prevent members of the group from acting as a unit. In either case, conflict weakens. Great or dangerous undertakings are to be avoided in times of conflict because achieving success requires a concerted unity of force.

During our lifetimes we will achieve many goals, some big, some small. It is good to know when the task is too monumental, and to back away. He is not wise who takes every turn.

In *I Ching Wisdom* it states:

> *If you attempt too much,*
> *you will end*
> *by succeeding*
> *in nothing.*

wu wei's comment:

It is commendable to push ourselves to new heights; we can thereby increase our strengths and reach ever greater successes. If, however, we strive to reach unrealistic or unattainable goals, we court disaster and failure and may lose even that which we already have. The superior person does not overreach himself, overspend himself, or strive foolishly. In that way he enjoys a lifetime of success.

Lastly, on the way to the achievement of our goals, we must always seek to strive for that which is highest and best within us. If we want to enjoy our goals once we have attained them, we must have attained them in the right way. For instance, there is no taste of a real victory if we have cheated to win. Therefore, it is essential that we always "polish our already bright virtues."

In *I Ching Wisdom* it states:

*If you neglect
your good qualities and virtues,
you will cease to be of value
to your friends and neighbors.
Soon,
no one will seek you out
or bother about you.*

wu wei's comment:

By nurturing our good qualities and virtues, we insure that our inner worth will be inexhaustible, like a spring of sparkling, clear water, and all will seek us out. The more that is drawn from us, the more that will remain and the greater will become our wealth. Those who understand these words will find them more precious than diamonds and gold.

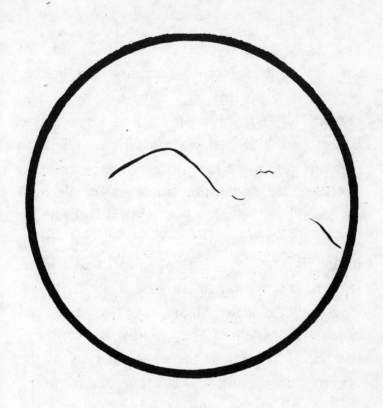

CHAPTER TWENTY-ONE

DEATH

Death is a transition. It is part of the flow of life. Everything comes from its opposite: to become small, something must first be big; to become big, something must first be small; to become cold, something must first be hot; to become hot, something must first be cold; to become dead, something must first be alive; to become alive, something must first be dead. If it were not that way, it would be the only thing in the Universe that did not follow that course. It is the alternation of life and death that, like the varying tones of music, gives harmony and beauty to existence. The coming and going of life and death mirror the ebb and flow of the oceans, the waxing and waning of the moon, the turning of the seasons, and all else in the Universe. Without death, life would become a bore.

In *I Ching Wisdom* it states:

> *To a person of true understanding*
> *it makes no difference*
> *whether death comes early or late.*

wu wei's comment:

A person of understanding cultivates himself and uses his time productively. His sense of the transitoriness of life does not impel him to uninhibited revelry to enjoy life while it lasts, nor to yield to melancholy and sadness, thereby spoiling the time remaining to him. Secure in the knowledge that all is one, he experiences himself as much a part of the universe as the stars and the trees, as enduring as All-That-Is. Knowing that time is only an illusion, he feels no break with time. Understanding that, you need have no fear of the moment of death, which is only a point of transition, such as walking through a doorway from one room into another and no more remarkable than any other moment.

It is unworthy of us to believe that our magnificent Universe that contains such beauty and grandeur would crown the ending of our lives with emptiness. Isn't it clear that death is part of life, that they go together, like winter and spring, that one is an extension of the other and that both are a part of the One?

That is the way: an endless progression, not toward perfection, but through perfection. Everything is always perfect. It is a state that we cannot depart from. The Universe is not flawed in any way. Relax. Be of good cheer. You have all of eternity within which to exist.

CHAPTER TWENTY-TWO

WORDS, DEEDS, AND INTENT

All actions are the blossoms of thought. Even the actions we think are spontaneous have been earlier decided in our minds. Whether our actions bring us good fortune or ill fortune is entirely dependent upon our intentions in carrying out the actions.

In *I Ching Wisdom* it states:

> *Through words and deeds*
> *the superior person*
> *moves*
> *heaven and earth.*

wu wei's comment:

By our words and deeds we create good fortune and misfortune. Therefore, shouldn't we be careful of what we say and do? All words and deeds spring from within. If our hearts are pure and our motivations that of the superior person, our words will be direct and powerful, and our actions will produce far reaching, beneficial effects. If our hearts are not as they should be, can anything else happen but that we fall into a pit of our own creation?

If we want to benefit ourselves as much as possible, we will see to it that our intentions are to benefit everyone and everything as much as possible. Natural law would then take care of the rest, bringing us inestimable benefits.

We all have consciences. They are there to protect us. They are built into us from the beginning. They are patterned after what is right in the Universe. When we act, or think about acting, we unconsciously compare our intended action to the Universal pattern of perfection in our minds. Then we form a judgment and act.

Some of us act contrary to what we know to be right. Sometimes we even enjoying doing it, believing we are benefiting ourselves. If we receive a benefit from acting against what we know to be right action, we unconsciously or consciously may decide to follow that new pattern the next time a similar situation arises. Ultimately, acting against what we know to be right, will, in the end, cause us to incur misfortune so that we will again set our feet upon the path of the superior person. That is why it states in the *I Ching*: "On the path of the superior person, there are always digressions, but you must turn back before going to far."

In *I Ching Wisdom* it states:

> You have received a nature
> that is innately good.
> When your thoughts and actions
> are in accord with your nature,
> you will enjoy
> great good fortune
> and supreme success.

wu wei's comment:

It is true that we are divine incarnations, perfect beings. When, however, we act out of greed, selfishness, meanness, hatred, or other such inferior motives, we act the part of lesser beings and so experience pain, despair, and frustration. Those feelings are only to let us know that we have departed from the path of the superior person. Feelings of love and joy let us know that we are on the path. Whatever we are experiencing is a result of our intentions, our thoughts, and our actions. It is we who are in charge of our fates, and not another.

Hatred can consume us if we indulge ourselves in that passion. Sometimes we use the word hatred casually. For instance, we say, "I hate the taste of castor oil." What we mean is that we intensely dislike the taste of castor oil. Hatred is what we feel for people or sometimes animals that have harmed us in some way or even a place where we have experienced great harm.

The effects we experience in our bodies when we feel hatred are exceptionally detrimental to us. Adrenaline pulses through our veins; we secrete all kinds of chemicals that the body produces in response to our hate, chemicals that destroy our bodies, put lines in our faces, and ruin the quality of life.

In *I Ching Wisdom* it states:

> *Do not hate.*
> *Hatred is a form of subjective involvement*
> *that binds you to the hated object.*

wu wei's comment:

> Hatred is a product of evil. To the extent we allow ourselves to feel hatred, to that extent we become instruments of evil. When we hate someone we draw that person to us. Is that what we want? To eliminate the connection, we only need to dismiss the person from our thoughts. To combat evil, we respond with goodness.

If we could cause the person we hate to disappear, we would. Well, we can essentially do that by dismissing that person from our thoughts. If the person is not in our thoughts, he may as well have disappeared.

To dismiss the person from our thoughts means that we consciously stop thinking about that person and replace the thoughts about that person with other thoughts. In other words, we think about something else. We may have to do that many times before thoughts of the person stop recurring in our minds, but be assured, the thoughts of that person will stop recurring in our minds, and we will then be free from the tyranny of our hatred.

Sometimes we feel hatred for another person because we have been told that the person has said bad things about us. That is particularly true if what the person said is untrue.

In *I Ching Wisdom* it states:

> *Slander*
> *will be silenced*
> *if*

*we do not gratify it
with injured retorts.*

wu wei's comment:

> We can spend a lifetime tracking down
> and defending ourselves against the
> negative things people say. It is better
> simply to go on with our own affairs. With
> nothing to keep the talk alive, it dies for
> lack of attention. The best defense
> against slander is to live the life of the
> superior person, letting our actions and
> conduct speak for us.

We have a choice about how we respond to
events, at least if we are in control of our
responses. When we allow ourselves to react
on the basis of our emotions rather than our
good judgment, we forfeit our choice.

In *I Ching Wisdom* it states:

> *To act on the spur of every caprice,
> ultimately
> leads to humiliation.*

wu wei's comment:

> What the heart desires, we run after
> without a moment's hesitation, but there
> are three restraints that ought to be given
> consideration: first, we should not run
> precipitately after all persons we would
> like to influence, but should hold back if it
> is unseemly for us to make an approach;
> second, we should not yield to every
> whim of those in whose service we are;
> third, where the moods of the heart are
> concerned, we should not ignore the
> possibility of inhibition, for this is the basis
> of human freedom. Develop the strength
> to choose a wise course of action even in
> the face of desires that pull you in a
> different direction. This is very difficult but
> essential if you are to be in charge of your
> fate, and leads to great success and good
> fortune.

Added to the above three restraints is a fourth
restraint: we should not act on the spur of every
emotion.

An excellent way to achieve the goal of correct thoughts and actions is to read about great deeds that have been done in the past and great sayings that have been handed down through the centuries. In that way we gain inspiration and provide ourselves with worthy heroes to help us in walking the path of the superior person.

In *I Ching Wisdom* it states:

> *A superior person*
> *acquaints himself with many sayings of*
> *antiquity*
> *and many deeds of the past,*
> *and thus strengthens his character.*

wu wei's comment:

By studying the sayings that have survived the test of the centuries, we gain wisdom. By learning of the deeds of our ancient heroes, we gain inspiration. Wisdom, coupled with inspiration, leads to great good fortune and supreme success.

CHAPTER TWENTY-THREE

THE SUPERIOR PERSON

Throughout the *I Ching* and this book, there are many references to "the superior person." The term refers to a person who acts with worthy motives, who strives to be the best person possible. Being that type of person brings the greatest rewards imaginable.

In *I Ching Wisdom* it states:

> *Every person*
> *must have something to follow,*
> *a lodestar.*

wu wei's comment:

Everyone needs something to bring out the best in himself and to provide direction for his development. By holding the image of the superior person in your mind as your lodestar, you will achieve not only supreme success but also great happiness.

It is of great benefit to know the qualities of the superior person. Listed below are a few of them.

He is humble.
He is willing to let others go ahead of him.
He is courteous.
His good manners stem from his humility and
    concern for others.
He is good-natured.
He is calm.
He is always inwardly acknowledging the
    wonder he feels for all of creation.
He is willing to give another the credit.
He speaks well of everyone, ill of no one.
He believes in himself and in others.
He does not swear.
He is physically fit.
He does not over-indulge.
He knows what is enough.
He can cheerfully do without.
He is willing to look within himself to find the
    error.

He is true to what he believes.

He is gentle.

He is able to make decisions and to act on them.

He is reverent.

He carries on his teaching activity.

He does not criticize or find fault.

He is willing to take the blame.

He does not have to prove anything.

He is content within himself.

He is dependable.

He is aware of danger.

He is certain of his right to be here.

He is certain of your right to be here.

He is aware that the Universe is unfolding as it should.

He is generally happy.

He laughs easily.

He can cry.

It is all right with him if another wins.

His happiness for another's happiness is sincere.

His sorrow for another's sorrow is sincere.

He has no hidden agendas.

He is thrifty, and therefore is not in want.

He finds a use for everything.

He honors everyone, and is therefore, honored.

He pays attention to detail.

He is conscientious.

He values everyone, and, therefore, everyone values him.

He is optimistic

He is trustworthy.

He is good at salvage.

He is patient.

He knows the value of silence.

He is peaceful.

He is generous.

He is considerate.

He is fair.

He is courageous in the face of fear.

He is clean.

He is tidy.

He does not shirk his duties.

He causes others to feel special.

He expects things to turn out well.

He is always seeking to benefit others in some
way.

His presence has a calming effect.

He is not attached to things.

He sees obstruction as opportunity.

He sees opposition as a signpost deflecting him
in the right direction.

He sets a good example.

He is joyous of heart.

He takes thought for the future.

He wastes nothing; therefore he always has
enough.

He has good manners.

He obtains nothing by force.

He overlooks the mistakes of others.

He has greatness of spirit.

He is clear headed.

He does more than his share.

He meets others more than half way.

He rests when it is time to rest; he acts when it
    is time to act.

He feels no bitterness.

He is forgiving.

He does not pretend.

He is not cynical.

He studies.

He reveres the ancient masters.

He is inspiring.

He nourishes nature and therefore is nourished
    by nature.

He leaves things better than he found them.

He does not make a show.

He practices goodness.

He is simple.

His intentions are always beneficial.

He is a wellspring of determination.

He does not boast.

He produces long lasting effects.

He has endurance.

He is flexible in his thinking.

He does not overreach himself.

He does not overspend himself.

He does not strive foolishly.

He is consistent.

He does not go into debt.

He lives a simple life.

He nurtures his good qualities and virtues.

He is sensitive to his inner promptings.

He exists in the present.

He feels no break with time.

He is cautious.

He is fit.

He is kind.

He holds his goals lightly in his mind, allows no opposing thoughts to enter and, as a result of natural law, is drawn inexorably to his goals.

He seeks enlightenment.

He sets limitations for himself within which he experiences complete freedom.

He is careful of his words, knowing he is reflected in them.

He does not use flattery.

He depends on himself for his happiness.

He feels secure.

He knows the truth of his existence.

He does not strive for wealth, fame, popularity or possessions.

He does not complain.

He turns back immediately having discovered that he has strayed from the path of the superior person.

He practices daily self-renewal of his character.

In *I Ching Wisdom* it states:

> *Only*
> *through daily self-renewal of character*
> *can you continue*
> *at the height of your powers.*

wu wei's comment:

It takes Herculean effort to reach the peak of perfection in any area of life and continuous effort to remain there. Every day some effort must be expended in refreshing ourselves with the ways of the superior person. Reading the *I Ching* or other great books, talking to like-minded people, teaching others, studying the deeds of our ancient heroes, thinking about our actions of the day to see whether we are being the best that we can be, all are ways to continue on the path. As we grow in awareness, our power will grow, and our attainments will be like the harvest after a perfect summer. There is no other activity that will reward us as richly as the daily self-renewing of our characters.

This is where I leave you, my friend. I am not leaving you in any real sense of the word, for there is no place to go. We are here, all of us, eternally. When everyone comes to know that, everyone will act in everyone's best interests. Remember that we are divine children of a golden Universe, as much a part of the Universe as the Universe itself.

May you learn quickly, benefit greatly, and attain to sublime wisdom. I wish you great good fortune, and may you mount to the skies of success as though on the wings of six dragons.

Your humble and insignificant servant,

-wu wei

INDEX

A Tale Of The I Ching, 8, 108
acknowledging the great
    Creator, 26
act on the spur of every caprice,
    218
AIDS, 92, 111
all is one, 36, 209
Alzheimer's, 92
anger, 37, 69, 72, 73, 115, 193
arbitrary choice, 84
atoms, 34

bad habits, 156, 157
bamboo skewers, 11
baseness, 41
bear with the mistakes of
    others, 177
beginning of a project, 199
beginnings, 106, 170
beware of becoming
    intoxicated, 168
Bible, 32
binary system, 7
birth, 31, 110
Bollingen Series XIX, ii, xix
bonus benefit, 91, 131
bright virtue, 43
business, 130, 162, 164, 165,
    168, 170, 171, 172, 174,
    176, 189

cancer, 92

cause and effect, x, 45, 47, 49,
    57, 67, 94, 136, 198
change, xiv, 10, 47, 89, 100,
    107, 108, 109, 110, 117,
    118, 129, 131, 147, 166,
    167
channeled, 9
chaos, 29, 30, 100, 112
character attribute, 43
Chou Shin, xvi, xvii
Christmas, 70, 74
combat evil, 216
come to terms with your
    opponent, 172
commitment, 63
communicate with that
    sparkling Universe, 25
complain, 130, 135, 140, 229
completely sincere, 80
concentration, 191, 192
concerned in thought, 60
conflict, 172, 173, 203, 204
conflict within, 204
confronted with insurmountable
    forces, 173
cork on the ocean, 91
correcting deficiencies, 71
Cory, 70, 71, 72, 73, 76
credit enslaves, 178

danger, 10, 16, 17, 18, 19, 72,
    95, 148, 172, 174, 178, 186,
    201, 204, 224

death, 15, 31, 32, 93, 110, 138, 208, 209, 210
decrease, 148, 152, 176
deeds of the past, 220
desire, 14, 36, 50, 124, 133
digressions, 22, 214
directness of mind, 89
divine being, 25, 114, 125, 144
DNA, 6, 8
do not be rigid and immobile, 166
drinking, xiii, 192, 193
Duke of Chou, xviii

eating, 160, 193
educators, 114
emperor, xiv, xvi
endings, 106
energy, 35, 36, 49, 84, 89, 98, 100, 101
enjoy a meaningful way of life, 66
enlightenment, 13, 14, 15, 16, 20, 60, 61, 228
entangled in a conflict, 172
eternal laws, xv
eternity, 15, 105, 144, 186, 210
every ending contains a new beginning, 106
evolution, 28, 31
exercises in meditation, 191
expenditures, 81, 178

fatal flaws, 78
fate, xv, 52, 53, 57, 59, 61, 62, 82, 92, 112, 215, 219
favorably inclined, 58, 93

fear, xvi, xvii, 28, 54, 69, 85, 88, 89, 90, 91, 92, 94, 115, 119, 131, 141, 182, 183, 202, 209, 225
financial matters, 178
flaw, 78, 170, 202
force, 1, 8, 55, 93, 147, 151, 191, 202, 203, 204, 226
form a decision, 171
fox crossing thin ice, 184
friends, 41, 50, 70, 84, 114, 115, 198, 206
Fu Hsi, xii, xiv, xv, xvii, 6, 8, 9, 108, 109, 110

Gai Tsung, xvii
game, 97, 100, 102, 103
garden, 54, 65
generosity, 182
gentleness, 119, 120, 182
gift of God, 56
glory of a king, 142
gluons, 34
goal, ix, x, 1, 14, 40, 41, 42, 63, 66, 67, 83, 118, 150, 168, 185, 196, 199, 200, 201, 202, 203, 222
God, 26, 29, 31, 32, 56, 97, 98, 99, 101
golden Universe, 60, 63, 230
goodness, 158, 216, 227
gravity, 101, 127
great harmony, 1, 39, 152
greatest deed, 4, 63
greatest gift of all, 144
greatness of spirit, 177, 226

halfway, 172

happiness, 28, 39, 40, 82, 183, 222, 224, 229
hardness, 34, 181
harvest, 132, 230
health, 50, 147, 148, 154, 155, 158, 159
heart desires, 219
hope, 91, 147, 148, 162, 192
humiliation, 198

I am not afraid of death, 15
I Ching way, 15
immortality, 32
in times of prosperity, 148
income, 50, 131, 178, 184, 185
increase, 148, 152, 157, 176, 189, 201, 205
indestructible child, 60, 63
injustice, 38
inner composure, 91, 159, 192
inner law of your being, 66
insecure, 67, 68, 198
integrity, 79, 88
intentional transgressions, 177
irritable people, 49

jealous, 67
job, 57, 76, 81, 94, 114, 117, 129, 130
joyful journey, 16
joyous of heart, 60, 226
justice, 121

key, xii, 9, 10, 55
King Wen, xvii, xviii
King Yu, xvii

kua, xiv, xv, xviii, 6, 8, 9, 10, 16, 17, 18, 55, 71, 72, 73, 76, 147, 148
kua 18, 71
kua 26, 73
kua 5, 17, 18, 55
kua 51, 17, 55

lied, 88
Lien San, xvii
lies, 88
life form, 27, 28, 33, 61
life in a stone, 33
light force, 147
light of eternity, 105
lodestar, 222
loss, 75, 79, 131, 138, 140, 147, 148, 152

mad pursuit of pleasure, 41
manifesting a humble attitude, 197
mate, 67, 68, 77, 80, 81, 84, 85, 86
mathematical model of the Universe, xiv
matter, 4, 28, 34, 35, 36, 40, 49, 60, 75, 77, 101, 106, 117, 127, 150, 165, 171, 197
meditation, 191, 192
misfortune, xii, 26, 114, 198, 201, 202, 212
modesty, 168, 198, 199
mold, 109
molecules, 34
motorcycle, 17

234

natural law, 14, 38, 53, 67, 81,
    125, 127, 133, 159, 228
neutrinos, 34
neutrons, 34
nine, 58, 59
nucleus, 34, 35

omniscience, 98, 99
on the wings of six dragons, 2,
    140, 231
oral tradition, xv

parents, 70, 72, 74, 114, 115,
    117, 122, 123, 127
partner, 68, 69, 70, 77, 79, 83,
    85, 86, 125, 164
partners, 65, 69, 70, 77, 79, 85
Pax, 29
perfect balance, 182
perfect hands of the Universe,
    15
person of true understanding,
    209
personal goals, 197, 198
physicist, 27
physics, 49
power, xi, 33, 99, 101, 120,
    121, 122, 126, 135, 171,
    196, 198, 203, 230
Power Press, i, ii, viii, 59
pretend love, 81
Princeton University Press, ii,
    xix
problem, 71, 77, 99, 124, 157,
    180, 190
prosperity, 60, 148, 177, 178
protons, 34
psychic body, 154

real estate, 18
real you, 70
recovery, 147
relationships, 67, 68, 70, 78, 79,
    82, 83, 84
religion, 31, 32
rest and movement, 188
retreat is proper, 173
reverent, 26, 27, 224
rewards of a prince, 142
rock, 54, 197
rules, 30, 69, 100, 103, 134

safe atmosphere, 68, 69
sage, xii, xiv, xviii, 93
sayings of antiquity, 77, 220
secret forces, 84
secure, 67, 68, 92, 229
self image, 46, 90, 115
selfishness, 181, 182, 215
separation, 29, 181
Shang Dynasty, xvi
shock, 17, 54, 56, 57
simplicity, 179
situation only becomes
    favorable, 139
six, xiv, 2, 6, 9, 58, 72, 140,
    147, 231
size of an atom, 35
small means, 179
small power, 196
soul life, 116
space, 35, 69, 107, 108
spider web, 13
stillness, 192, 193, 194
stimulation, 37
stubbed toe, 93
sublime success, 16, 39, 47

superior person, x, xii, 14, 15,
22, 26, 38, 41, 42, 43, 47,
50, 52, 57, 60, 80, 81, 82,
84, 91, 105, 112, 120, 121,
134, 140, 141, 142, 143,
148, 150, 157, 158, 159,
163, 165, 166, 170, 173,
177, 178, 179, 182, 186,
189, 193, 200, 202, 205,
212, 214, 215, 218, 220,
222, 223, 229, 230

Tan, xviii
tap on the shoulder, 52, 54
telling the truth, 88
three restraints, 219
thrift, 81
Tiffany, 70, 71, 72, 73, 74, 75,
76
time, xiv, xv, xvi, xvii, 9, 17,
19, 21, 27, 34, 37, 61, 74,
79, 84, 88, 89, 91, 107, 108,
110, 111, 117, 118, 136,
138, 143, 147, 148, 149,
151, 157, 170, 171, 173,
174, 176, 186, 188, 189,
191, 198, 203, 204, 209,
214, 227, 228
tiny hairline, 105
transition, 208, 209
transitory, 105, 106, 144
travel in the energy field, 36

tree on a mountain, 163
true missions, 125
true nature, 1, 93, 151

understanding of fate, xv
Universe is favorably inclined,
58
Universe is not flawed, 210
unkindness, 38
unlimited possibilities, 186

virtue, 43, 73, 143
void, 109, 110, 111
volatile, xi

warrior, 15
wealth, 176, 180, 182, 183,
184, 185, 186, 198, 206,
229
Wen, xvi, xvii, xviii
Who We Think We Are, 46, 47,
48
work, 68, 72, 73, 84, 129, 130,
131, 132, 135, 155, 162,
183, 184, 199
workout situation, 61, 90
writing, xv, 7, 11, 107

yarrow stalks, viii, 11, 45, 59,
118, 130
Yu, xvii